ˈpraktikəl

Ideas for the real world

"If you love Design Thinking and are struggling to help others see the potential, you are not alone – and this book is for you! Many Design Thinking professionals are so passionate about our craft, we find it frustrating when others don't see it the same way. And we are left scratching our heads, wondering "what's wrong with these people". But the truth is each one of us needs to have our own "Aha! moment" before we can become a believer. And there is a significant difference between being a great Design Thinking Practitioner and being a successful Design Thinking Champion.

In his new book, "How Might We Champion Design Thinking in Your Organization?", Dan Buchner strikes right at the heart of these challenges. And he equips readers with practical and actionable ways to help other people in their organization see the benefits of Design Thinking and join the cause. I read the whole book in one sitting. And I can't wait to share it with my Design Thinking colleagues. Thank you, Dan, for shedding light on some fantastic tools that I know I will use again and again."

- **AMY HEDRICK**, *Senior Director, Experience Design, Fusion 360 at Autodesk*

"When I brought Design Thinking to my team, I didn't have a resource like Dan's book. His approach would have made the transformation a hundred times easier. Dan's book is full of real-world examples, tips and tricks (many of which worked for me!), insights and ideas. With this book as your guide, you'll be in a better place to bring Design Thinking into your organization and make long-lasting change happen."

- **TRINA WELLENDORF**, *Learning Experience Design Team Lead at Accenture*

"Once I started reading How Might We I couldn't put it down! I really enjoyed the format—the story followed by the so-what, then some really practical ideas. It's a guide for changing mindsets and shifting organizational and individual perceptions. And, the HMW questions are great prompts to challenge our own thinking. It's a book I'll give my peers to help them continue their journey with design thinking."

- **SARAH X**, *Passionate Design Thinking Champion,*
  (at an undisclosed multi-national financial services company)

"Dan connected with me, clearly describing the challenges I face. I felt like he was sitting across the table having a conversation with me, walking me through how to bring design thinking to my organization. His real-world stories kept me reading."

- **FRANKIE ITURBE**, *Education Entrepreneur – WeElevate, Technology Consulting Manager - Accenture*

"Empathetic designer, consummate coach, and passionate believer in the power of a thoughtful open-ended question, Dan Buchner provides an enlightened and practical platform for the Champions of Design Thinking. His connective and illustrative style brings to life revelations of experiences as a Corporate Innovator and Design Thinking consultant. The book, like the man, brings clarity and hope to designing purposeful conversations, listening with intent, putting others' needs first, and the power of collaboration, alignment and mutual success. How Might We is thoughtfully told and designed to live on the desk of every Design Thinking Champion for the rest of their lives. Not just their work life, but their complete life."

- **KORY KOLLIGIAN**, *Former COO, EPAM Continuum*

"This book is a must-have for any Design Thinkers facing big, complex barriers on a regular basis. Dan has the ability to distill the purest form of design thinking tools and offer them in a direct yet approachable, practical, non-academic way. For those of us who don't find the time to read yet another business book written by some consultant who speaks about everything in the ideal state, How Might We offers a refreshing look at what happens when things are not successful. It urges us to celebrate those times — talk about them, learn from them, build our personal confidence from them."

- **SUSAN EICK**, *CEO, The Refinery Leadership Partners*

"This book beautifully integrates what in design we call turning thinking and doing into being; a particular mindset that becomes a liberating force from the ordinary, well-established, and restricted ways of thinking, behaving, and going about life in general. Dan shares with us a synthesis of thought and action based on his fruitful and caring perspective, built on many, many years working with others. In a guided format, this book helps us discover possibilities by providing us with proven-to-work best practices for change."

- **EDUARDO MILRUD**, Ph.D. *Studio Lead, Design, Savanah College of Art & Design*

"This is the book that we all need in order to help us champion innovation and unlock what is possible. We learn even more about design thinking through Dan's real-world business examples, and the many practical tools he provides. Dan brings so much wisdom and experience to the stories he shares – not to mention a great sense of humour— making the book a fun and incredibly engaging read. Dan's passion for helping others and his generosity in sharing what he knows is inspirational. Thanks to this phenomenal book, we are more empowered to bring our design thinking mindset and toolkit to the next opportunity, while helping others embrace the value of this human-centred approach."

- **JOANNA KIRKE**, *CEO, Kirke Leadership Inc.*

FriesenPress

Suite 300 - 990 Fort St
Victoria, BC, V8V 3K2
Canada

www.friesenpress.com

Foreword: Chris Pacione, CEO & Co-Founder LUMA Institute LLC

Editing and Proofing: Lina Branter, www.linabcontent.com

Book and Cover Design: Deborah LeFrank and Suzanne DuQuesnay, Visual Life Stories Ltd. www.visuallifestories.com

Illustrations and Lettering: Deborah LeFrank, Visual Life Stories Ltd.

Author Photograph: Lauren Buchner, www.laurens-studio.com

Creative Direction: Dan Buchner

DiSC® is a registered trademark of Inscape Publishing. Myer-Briggs Indicator® and MBTI® are trademarks or registered trademarks of the Myers-Briggs Indicator Trust in the United States and other countries. StrengthsFinder® is a registered trademark of The Gallup Organization.

Disclaimer
While the publisher and the author have used their best efforts in preparing this book, the material in this publication is of a nature of general comment only, and does not represent professional advice. It is not intended to provide specific guidance for particular circumstances and should not be relied on as basis for any decision to take action or not take action on any matter which it covers. Readers should obtain professional advice where appropriate, before making any decision. To the maximum extent permitted by law, the author and publisher disclaim all responsibility and liability to any person, arising directly or indirectly from any person taking or not taking action based on the information in this publication.

ISBN
978-1-03-911095-3 (Paperback)
978-1-03-911097-7 (eBook)

1. *Business & Economics, Decision-Making & Problem Solving*

Distributed to the trade by The Ingram Book Company

To Lauren, *the love of my life*.

And to

Aaron and Stef,
Zach and Janel,
Elliot and Judd.

ACKNOWLEDGEMENTS

To all those who taught me so much throughout my journey.

Noelle Dye, a true pioneer of design research and visionary thinker. Thank you for pushing me to think bigger. Without your insights this book could not have happened.

Kory Kolligian, the master of fostering human-centered organizational cultures. Thank you for showing me that leading a successful business is all about the people.

Freda King, the quiet provocateur. Thank you for prodding me to stay focused on people every day.

Allan Cameron, the wise one. Thank you for helping me get real with myself so I could be real with others.

David Knapp-Fisher, the author and inspirational speaker. Thank you for the practical advice on getting this book written and out into the world.

To all those who played a role in making this book a reality.

Lina Branter, for your expert editing and proof reading.

Deborah LeFrank, for your creative insights and illustrations.

Suzanne DuQuesnay, for your inspired graphic design skills.

Chris Pacione, for taking the time to review an early draft and write the foreword.

Amy Hedrick, **Beth Brewer**, **Eduardo Milrud**, **Frankie Itrube**, **Joanna Kirke**, **Kory Koligian**, **Max Rowland**, **Sarah X** (you know who you are), **Susan Eick** and **Trina Wellendorf** for your encouragement, feedback and kind words.

FOREWORD

How Might We...isn't a book for your bookshelf. It is a book that wants (and literally asks) to be by your side; whether that is on your nightstand, in that small pile of texts stacked on the edge of your desk or tucked away in your backpack. It is one of those books that doesn't really want to be a book so much as a trusted guide and dog-eared companion, a book you can call on when you run into the inevitable obstacles that prevent your peers and clients from seeing the value of design thinking, and using it effectively in their everyday work.

At LUMA Institute, we believe in the words of the great Herb Simon; "Everyone designs who devises courses of action aimed at changing existing situations into preferred ones." The company I lead was founded to unveil and share the power of design with anyone who wants to work this way. Even so, we are quite realistic about the limitations of design thinking and are fully aware of the natural skepticism that many who are new to it or failed using it, may harbor.

And herein lies why you need this book and can trust this book. In spite of your passion and personal belief in design thinking, you will need help in overcoming the numerous personal and organizational causes for its resistance. Who better to help you with that than someone who has experienced and overcome this resistance?

Dan Buchner has been applying design thinking principle—and teaching and encouraging others to apply them—for years. And as you will see, he is very generous when it comes to sharing his own stories of success and failure, as well as the insights and ideas those experiences afforded him. He understands what design thinking is, and what it isn't. He knows first-hand how it can supercharge a team and help them become highly effective collaborators and creative problem solvers. But he also knows that design thinking is not some silver bullet that will magically end our struggles with teamwork and innovation.

And that is what you want from a guide (book) like this: A treatise authored by an authentic and generous authority. Dan gives you that in How Might We... because what he has to share is steeped in reality, and how he shares it is inspired by a passion to reach out and be of service to others.

Chris Pacione
CEO & Co-Founder
LUMA Institute

Why I wrote this book.

You. You're the reason I wrote this book. I have met so many like you. People who work in organizations big and small. People passionate about the potential of Design Thinking but who struggle to practice it in their organizations. I have met you while working together on projects, facilitating Design Thinking workshops, teaching in university programs, and lecturing in design schools around the world. What I hear you say is "Dan, how do I overcome the resistance to Design Thinking I face in my organization?"

This book is for you.

I've been a champion of this way of working long before someone coined the term Design Thinking. My work has taken me to 35 countries, inside all kinds of organizations, and across the domains of design, leadership, organizational change, and education. I have seen plenty of what works and what doesn't. I've had successes and failures. But I have persevered because I know the potential of Design Thinkers like you. You can make your organization a more creative and humane workplace to drive its success. You can create innovative solutions to complex problems we face in this world.

Being a champion of Design Thinking isn't easy. Organizations are complex and people are people. This book is my attempt to inspire you. To provide you with practical ideas to consider, try, and build on. It's a starting point. You must find what works in your situation, in your organization.

Thank you for taking up the challenge. We need more Design Thinking champions like you.

DAN BUCHNER

AN EXTENSIVE AND DETAILED TABLE OF CONTENTS

DESIGN THINKERS KNOW INNOVATIVE IDEAS RESULT FROM:

Hearing people's **Stories**.

Making **Observations** of people's behaviors.

Gaining fresh **Insights** into people's underlying motivations and desires.

Framing new **Opportunities** in the form of How Might We questions.

Brainstorming an expansive set of creative **Ideas** to test and iterate.

THAT'S HOW ALL THE FOLLOWING STORIES ARE ORGANIZED!

Change is uncomfortable and a constant struggle.

 Being passionate about Design Thinking isn't enough.

 Embrace the Champion's struggle?

 Championing Design Thinking means embracing risk.

 Be clear on our relationship with failure?

 Showing confidence builds other's confidence.

HMW... Give ourselves 100% permission to be the expert?

 Championing Design Thinking is a marathon, not a sprint.

HMW... Fuel our persistence?

 Rejection is an opportunity to get curious.

HMW... Not take it personally?

 **People dismiss what I'm saying.**

 **People won't embrace what they can't understand.**

HMW... **Speak in their language?**

 **People listen for what is important to them.**

HMW... **Make words that matter?**

"IT'S NOT THE HORSE YOU'RE RIDING. IT'S HOW YOU'RE RIDING IT."

People don't see it my way.

aha! There are reasons why they're resisting.

HMW... Meet them where they are?

"I CAN'T GET SUPPORT TO TRY SOMETHING ELSE. I'M STUCK."

People want proof.

aha! Nothing is more convincing than success.

HMW... Get success to speak for itself?

People won't even try.

aha! It's easier for people to use the familiar than try the unfamiliar.

HMW... Become the familiar?

- Make it Everyday
- Slip into a Struggle
- Infiltrate the Tried and True
- Engage a Higher Power
- Draw Attention
- Go it Alone
- Design Thinking Wallpaper

Some people are really frustrating.

aha! It's not what's right for *you* that matters most.

HMW... Make *them* right?

- Yes And Judo
- Right-Right
- Assess and Flex
- Right Track
- Double Diamond is Your Best Friend

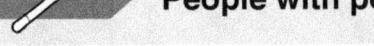

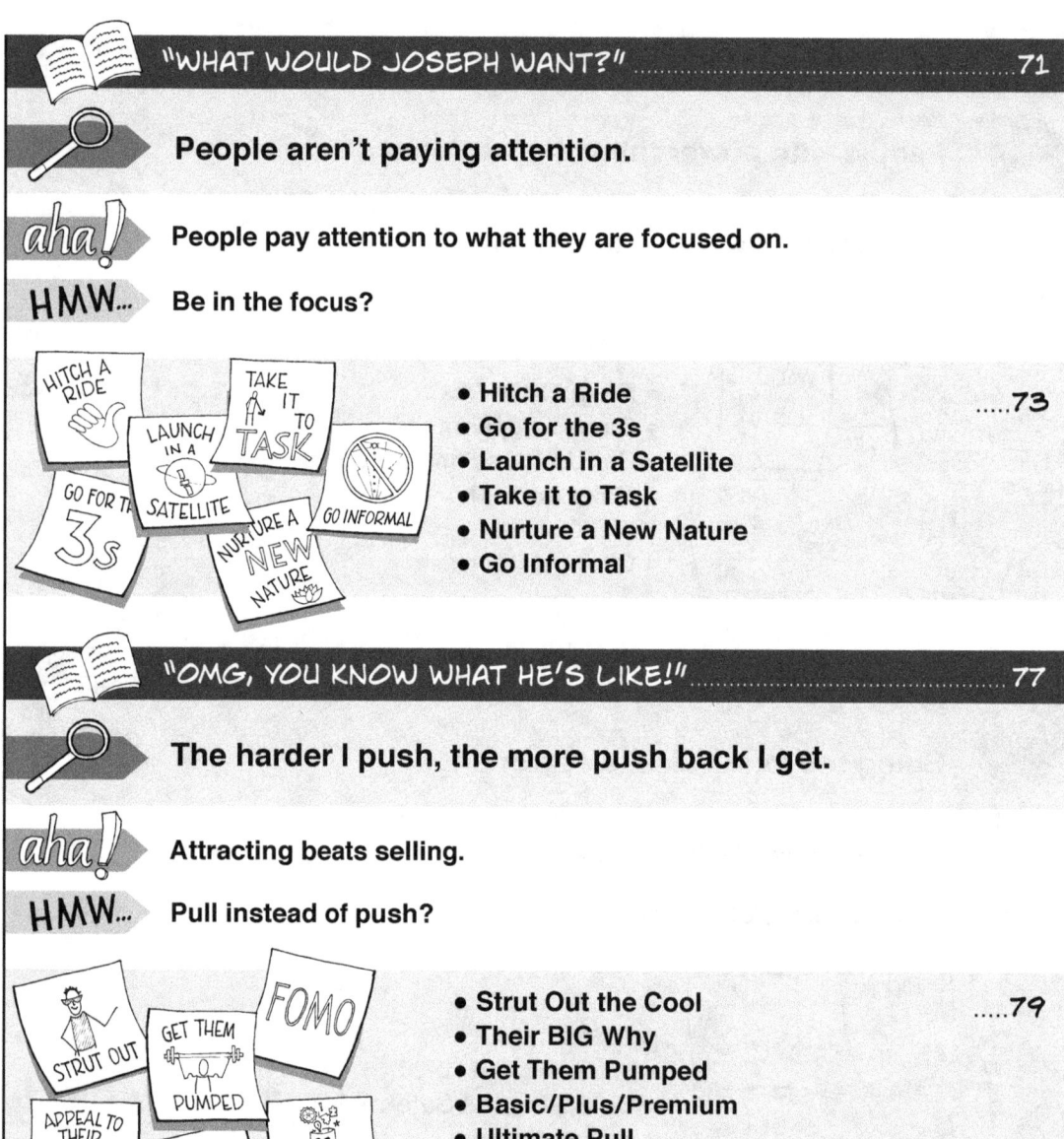

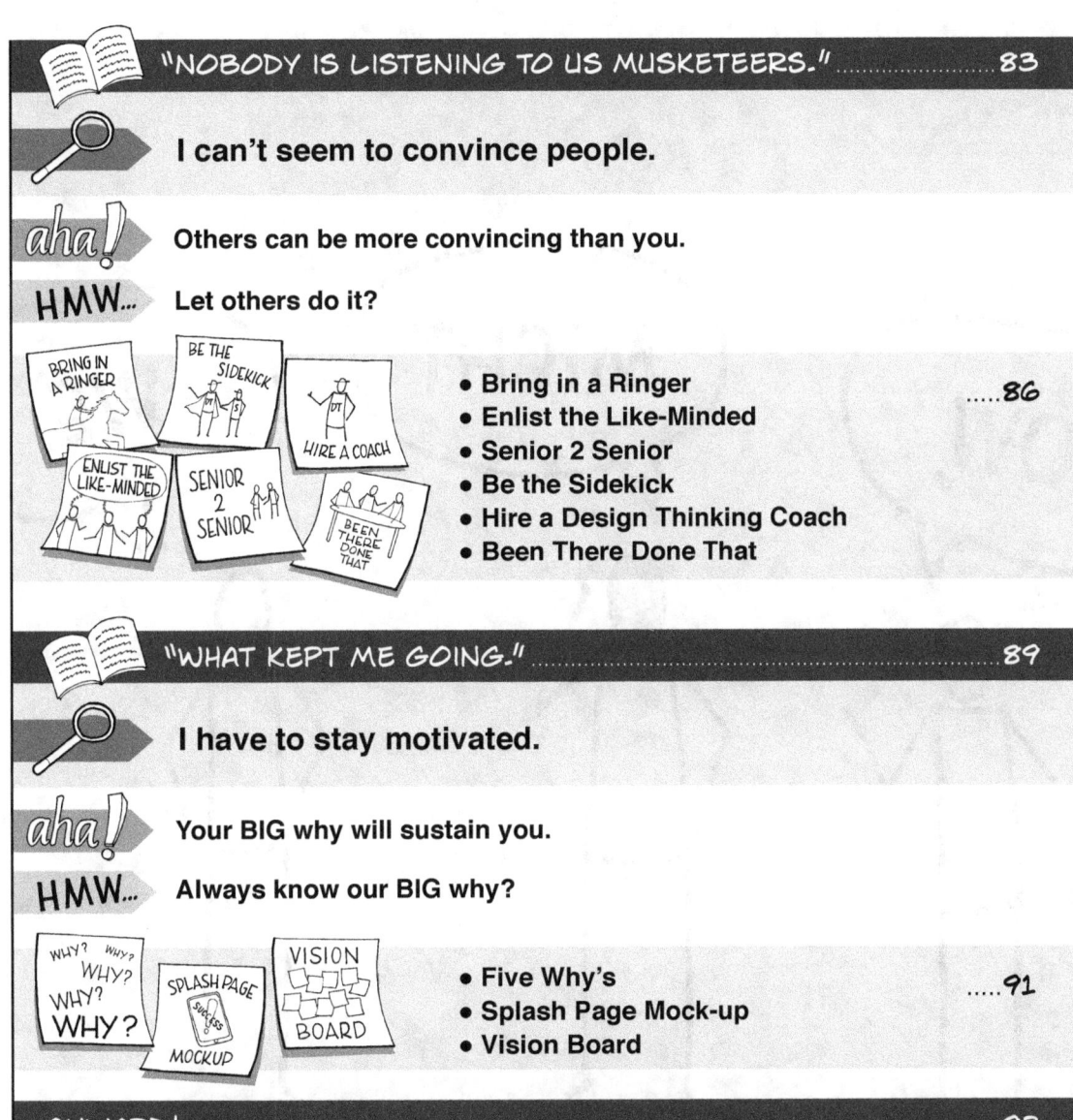

I'm glad you are reading this book. It means you're taking steps to fulfill your dream of having Design Thinking practiced in your organization. You believe it can make a big difference. Because you care deeply, the resistance you face – the leaders who don't get it, unwilling teammates, rigid policies and procedures – frustrate you. You're putting in a lot of effort, but don't feel you're making progress. I've been there. I know the challenges you face. It's daunting, but I can tell you it's doable. You have the passion and creativity. What you need are some practical ideas for championing Design Thinking in your organization.

I believe the <u>How Might We</u> (HMW) question is one of the most powerful methods in a Design Thinker's toolkit. HMW opens our thinking to possibilities. That is the spirit of this book.

HOW – *invites us to be practical. To focus us on getting to solutions.*

There are lots of books on how to do Design Thinking. How to do research, draw <u>insights</u>, generate ideas, <u>prototype and test</u>. How to apply Design Thinking in business, non-profits, government, and to big complex social issues. This book assumes you have read those. If you haven't, I've underlined key <u>Design Thinking</u> and <u>organizational change</u> concepts. You can find definitions and other helpful information in the Glossary. You may be fresh out of school or a seasoned practitioner, but you already have Design Thinking chops.

This is a different *How to* book. It is a practical guide on how to get the support you need. How to engage people to collaborate with you. How to encourage people to take a risk and try Design Thinking. How to overcome resistance. **This is a book on how to be a champion of Design Thinking**.

MIGHT – *gives us the permission to imagine a range of ideas.*

The ideas in this book are practical. They come from years of trial and error working with actual people in all kinds of organizations. Some ideas result from stunning successes. Others from the tough learning that comes from spectacular failures. You must try the ones that seem right for you. Are you trying to make people aware of Design Thinking? Are you trying to get those who are interested to learn more? Are you trying to get others to work with you in applying Design Thinking? Are you trying to make Design Thinking a major part of your organization's work processes? Or are you just trying to maintain enthusiasm in the face of stiff resistance? If so, there are ideas in this book for you.

WE – *reminds us to collaborate with others and imagine the best ideas together.*

Are you a solo Design Thinker, a project manager, a team facilitator, a manager of an innovation lab, a consultant, or a leader in your organization? Regardless of your position and perspective, being a champion means working with others. It's all about people. View this book as a collaboration between you and me. If at first an idea doesn't seem to fit in your situation, then "yes and" me. Take it and build on it. Let's work together to spark a new idea that might.

Capture your ideas and thoughts in spaces you'll find throughout this book.

Champion – *Noun: a person who fights for a cause.*
Verb: to support and defend a cause.

This book is about both the noun and the verb. It contains ideas on how to fight for the cause. It also contains **ideas on how to be a champion**. A champion's success results from the reinforcing relationship between the *be* and the *do*. Fortifying your confidence and increasing your influence is as important as executing tactics to build awareness and collaborating with allies. They work hand in hand. Mash up the best *be* and *do* ideas and make them work for you.

Design Thinking – *The human-centered approach we are all so passionate about.*

Some view Design Thinking as a process. For me, it's much more than that — it's a mindset needed to skillfully use a set of methods. Yes, the mindset and methods are used in the five stages of the <u>Design Thinking process</u>. And we can use them in championing too. You'll find some ideas in this book look really familiar!

Just as Design Thinking is anchored in a deep understanding of people, their struggles and aspirations, the ideas in this book begin with people. They come from insights gained in real-life experiences. And I have the stories to prove it! I share the ones where I learned the most. I also base the practical ideas on a set of guiding principles derived from research on why people resist change and what leads people to adopt alternative ways of working.

Your Organization

Organizations come in all sizes. They exist in a wide range of sectors. They have an array of different cultures. Some have been around for decades and some are brand new. They are complex and ever changing. I find Design Thinkers at all levels in organizations. They play all kinds of roles. This means there's no "Three Easy Steps" for championing Design Thinking. Every champion and every organization are unique. Because of this, there are a variety of ideas in this book. Some are small acts to bolster your confidence. Some are big initiatives requiring the support of senior leaders. And many are in between. Some may directly apply. Some may not. Use the ones that don't as inspiration to spark new ideas that fit you and your organization.

That's why I called this book, How Might We Champion Design Thinking in Your Organization!

HOW TO USE THIS BOOK

This book starts with developing an understanding of the <u>landscape</u>. We explore why the very nature of organizations makes it difficult for Champions like you, why people resist change and strategies for getting people to adopt alternate approaches. I summarized this in the **Guiding Principles for Design Thinking Champions**.

The remaining stories each follow a Design Thinker's approach:

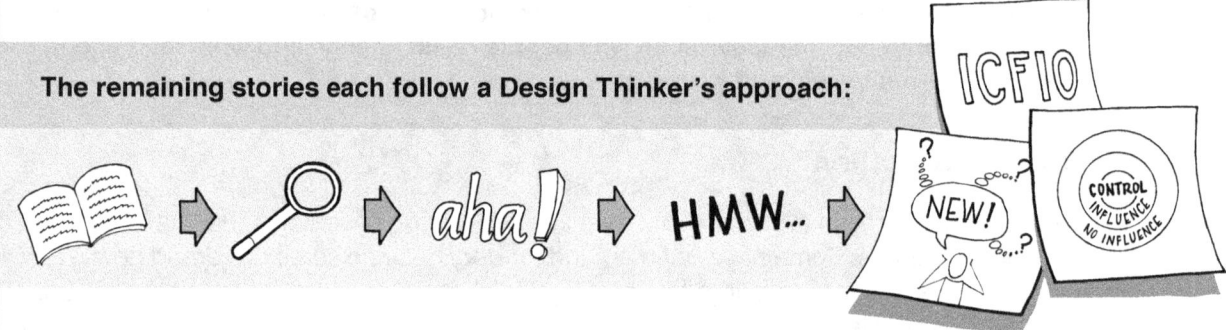

First, we start with listening to and observing people. Uncovering their experiences in real-life situations by hearing their **Stories**. I use stories of actual experiences I've had as a Design Thinking champion (names have been changed to protect the innocent!). Stories of my attempts to overcome the kinds of real-life struggles you face. From those stories I make key **Observations**. Some may be like ones you have made in your efforts to champion Design Thinking. *Next*, I draw **Insights** from the observations. Try to draw additional ones yourself. Insights are where the magic starts to happen. *Then*, based on those insights, I frame **Opportunities** in the form of How Might We questions. These are open-ended questions to inspire our imaginations. *And finally*, I share **Ideas** to address those HMW's. Ideas that have worked for me. Ideas you can try. Ideas you can build on to address the reality of your organization. Ideas to spark entirely new ideas.

The Design Thinking Champion's Struggle is foundational. Be sure to read it first. The stories that follow can stand on their own. There's lots of information in the **Table of Contents** to help you navigate. Here are some ways you can use this book:

- **Old-Fashioned** – Read it cover to cover. Enough said.

- **Interesting Stories** – We know the power of a good story. Look for the stories that catch your eye. See how they resonate (or not) with your situation.

- **Similar Observations** – Look for observations similar to ones you have made in your efforts to champion Design Thinking. See what insights, opportunities and ideas follow.

- **Go for the Insights** – Find the Insights that relate to the challenges you face. See if their HMW's and ideas might work for you.

- **HMW's** – Maybe you know the opportunity you're focused on and just want some ideas. Find the HMW that best describes it and go from there.

- **Affinity Clusters** – Each story contains an affinity cluster of ideas. Together these clusters address the bigger opportunity—HMW Champion Design Thinking in Your Organization. Scan all the clusters on pages 106-107 for patterns and inspiration, like you would a whiteboard full of sticky notes.

- **Investigate the Principles** – The Guiding Principles for Design Thinking Champions are outlined on page 12. As you read the book, pay attention to how they play out. Uncover ways those principles might inform your ideas.

- **Straight to Ideas** – We Design Thinkers are wary of going right to ideas, but nothing is stopping you from starting with the ideas that seem most interesting to you.

And remember, I have underlined key Design Thinking and organizational change concepts throughout the book. You can find definitions and other helpful information in the Glossary.

Now it's all up to you!

5

CELEBRATE!

+ LANGUAGE

STRUT OUT

ENGAGE A HIGHER POWER

SIDE HUSTLE

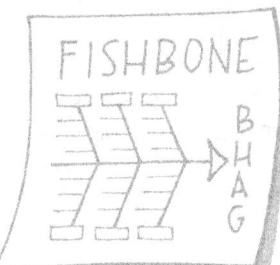

FISHBONE B H A G

LAUNCH IN A SATELLITE

EMPATHY MAP
THINK
HEAR SAY
FEEL
PAIN GAIN

VISION BOARD

MAKE A CASE

BE THE SIDEKICK

CAMEO APPEARANCE

1ST ROUND PICK

RIGHT!

OVERCOME A HURDLE

A DESIGN THINKING CHAMPION'S STRUGGLE

I hear Design Thinkers saying "My performance measures are not aligned with working in this way," or "I don't have the numbers to prove my idea yet but I know it's a great one," or "Will I ever be able to really use Design Thinking in my company?" Why do Design Thinkers struggle? There are two basic reasons: the very nature of organizations and people's resistance to change.

So, what is it about organizations?

I think of organizations as ecosystems: an interconnected tangle of people and processes working together towards a common goal. People in a non-profit organization work hard to provide services to people in need. They must show results or they will lose the support of their funders. People in a for-profit corporation must show sales and profit growth while minimizing the risk of legal liabilities and maximizing shareholder return. People working in a government must provide valuable services to its citizens or risk being voted out. Organizations are ecosystems finely tuned to produce reliable results at minimal risk. Because of this, rapid decision-making, quantitative proof, reliance on precedence, strictly defined roles, and adherence to proven processes are what's valued. These values become "just the way we do things around here."

Enter Design Thinking — an unfamiliar way of working; the creative, collaborative and human-centered approach we all love. As Design Thinkers, we reframe the problem given to us. We try things before we know we have the right answer. We view "failure" as learning. We set precedence aside to explore new, unproven solutions. We rely on our intuition. We work to break down departmental silos. Design Thinking with its inherent ambiguities and uncertainty runs headlong into the very nature of our organization. It's an invasive species, a creative intruder in a rational ecosystem. No wonder we champions are constantly struggling.

Why are some people so resistant to Design Thinking?

Organizations are comprised of people. Their attitudes, beliefs, and behaviors embody the values of their organization. That's why I hear Design Thinkers say, "The leaders in my organizations don't get it!" or "I'll never get my team to agree to work this way." Or "They just don't think the way I do." Not only are you working against the very nature of your organization, you are asking people to adopt an alternative way of working. This requires a change in some of their attitudes, beliefs, and behaviors. Change is hard for any of us. And getting others to change is a whole lot harder. Why? Because people resist change for seemingly good reasons. Have you asked yourself the following questions when faced with adopting an unfamiliar way of working?

What's in it for me?

How will this affect my role? Will I be more successful? What do I stand to gain from trying?

We are all self-centered when faced with trying something unfamiliar. Not that we are all selfish. We just naturally look for what might benefit us. You know Design Thinking can benefit your organiztion, but how can it benefit someone you need support from? You must show them *what's in it for them*. You need an understanding of what drives that person's behaviors; what are they passionate about? What does success look like for them? Then show them how practicing Design Thinking can help them achieve their goals.

What do I stand to lose?

What if it doesn't work? Will it affect my reputation?
Will people lose confidence in me?

For us humans, losses loom larger than gains. They call this the <u>loss avoidance bias</u> first showed by psychologists Amos Tversky and Daniel Kahneman. Losing social status, promotion opportunity, funding, etc. feels worse than gaining the same thing. Kahneman says, "Roughly speaking, losses hurt about twice as much as gains make you feel good." Paradoxically, when we ask ourselves, "What's in it for me?" we may well be thinking, "What do I stand to lose?" Showing the gains Design Thinking can produce is important. However, helping people avoid losses is even more powerful in getting them on board.

Why fix what's not broken?

Why change? It's always worked for me. Why change when I've been successful?

The current approach feels safe and predictable. The unfamiliar feels risky and unpredictable. Changing one's approach requires personal risk and effort. *How long will it take me to learn? Will I be able to actually do it? Will it work better than the way I do things now?* No wonder we resist trying the unfamiliar! So why would we do it? Too many organizations have rested on their laurels only to have lost it all. Success can breed complacency, and that's dangerous! You must show the advantage of being more creative, collaborative and customer focused. Sometimes what at first appears to be the riskier approach is the less risky way to succeed.

Why should I trust you when you say it will work?

So, you are asking me to try something unfamiliar?
This seems risky to me. I'm not sure.

As you know, change means increased risk. We humans determine the level of risk by assessing how uncertain we are and how vulnerable we feel; the more uncertain and the more vulnerable, the higher the risk. Building trust can increase people's willingness to take a higher risk. Helping lower their perceived uncertainty and vulnerability builds their trust in you.

What does it take to get people to adopt a new way?

We humans are a funny lot. We don't like change, yet we like the new. The latest mobile phone; the newest app; today's fashion. We like the new but resist change. Why is this?

Well, we do an internal calculation and make a deliberate decision to adopt the new or not. It's a simple equation: do the positive consequences of adopting the new outweigh the negative ones? Is the cost of the new phone outweighed by the cool factor of owning it? As Design Thinkers, we need to influence that calculation. E. M. Rogers, a professor of communications studies, gives us an excellent guide in his diffusion of innovation theory. He identifies five strategies for affecting people's decision to adopt a new way. I have adapted them for Design Thinking champions.

1. Show the relative advantage over the current options.

Design Thinking is often competing with approaches such as Agile, Stage Gate, and Waterfall. You need to show it is better in ways that are compelling. Is your organization's goal to be customer-focused? Get results faster? Lower the costs? Come up with more creative solutions? Whatever the goal, show how Design Thinking is better at achieving it than "the way things are done around here."

2. Ensure the new is compatible with what they value.

Show how Design thinking is consistent with an individual's values: desire for personal status, efficiency, being heard, making progress. Describe how Design Thinking aligns with your organization's values and mission and that it is key to achieving your organization's vision.

3. Reduce complexity to make the new way easy to understand and use.

People are unlikely to adopt something they don't understand or they find difficult to use. Simplify the Design Thinking concepts. Express them in ways they can comprehend. Make them accessible and easy to try.

4. Allow them to trial the new way before committing to it.

Make it easy for people to experience Design Thinking firsthand before asking for their full support. Give them a proverbial taste before they order the meal, the first month free before signing up for a yearly subscription.

5. Make the results visible.

Give people a look at what's possible with Design Thinking. Illustrate the benefits of increased customer focus, collaboration, and creativity. Use comparisons, before and after, testimonials. Highlight the successes both big and small.

WHAT DO YOU THINK?

There are powerful forces working against a Design Thinking Champion: the very nature of organizations and people's resistance to change. Here are principles to guide you in overcoming these forces. You'll find they underlie all the ideas in this book.

GUIDING PRINCIPLES FOR DESIGN THINKING CHAMPIONS

☐ Show people what's in it for them when they use Design Thinking.

☐ Demonstrate how Design Thinking can help them avoid losses.

☐ Expose the risks of not using Design Thinking.

☐ Build their trust by increasing their certainty and confidence.

☐ Highlight the relative advantage of Design Thinking over current approaches.

☐ Show Design Thinking is consistent with the organization's values.

☐ Make Design Thinking easy for people to understand and use.

☐ Allow people to try Design Thinking before they commit to it.

☐ Show tangible results Design Thinking can produce.

It's easy to say "show that Design Thinking is consistent with someone's values" or "increase their certainty and confidence." But it's not always clear how to actually do that. How do you show alignment with someone else's values? How do you increase someone's confidence?

Principles are great, but what you really need are some practical ideas and concrete actions you can take in your quest to champion Design Thinking in your organization.

So, here we go!
Let's start with a story.

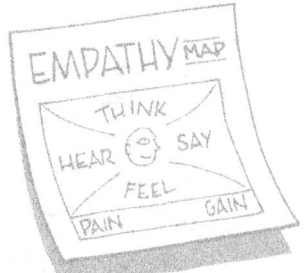

"This is your brain on new," Jamar said as he clicked to his second slide at our monthly staff meeting. He was responsible for business development at our design firm, and had been sounding the alarm of intensifying price pressure from our competitors. To stay a leader in the design world, he needed us to step up to the edge, the leading edge, and pioneer fresh approaches that could command top dollar. Up to that point our attempts were half-hearted at best. It was time consuming. It took extra effort. It was uncomfortable. It was easier to just keep doing what we did best. We were pros after all. We were successful. But Jamar's alarm bells were getting louder. Begrudgingly, we accepted we needed to try.

The brilliance of Jamar's "now to new" was the way he described how it would feel for each of us personally. Moving from "I got this" to "I feel like fraud". He wanted us to know if we weren't feeling the discomfort, we weren't really trying anything new.

After the meeting people asked, "How are we going to do this? How are we going to move from *now* to *new*?" My answer? Something I have said throughout my career: "We'll figure it out. Let's give ourselves permission to try, to risk failure in the attempt to develop new and unknown expertise. Why not have every team try something new and bold on each new project? Try novel ways to conduct research, generate ideas, prototype and test or interact with our clients? It doesn't matter. Just try one new thing. See if it works."

And that's what we did. Not everything we tried worked. Did having our brains on new make our heads hurt? Of course! But we persevered anyway. With each "failure" we picked ourselves up and made another attempt. We practiced the Design Thinker's creed, "build to learn".

Our willingness to put our brains on new and just figure it out showed us what we were capable of. Continually advancing our expertise became not only exciting, but expected. Ultimately, it kept us in a leadership position in our field and led to better client relation-ships, elevated brand reputation, and unprecedented financial performance. **Jamar's your brain on new showed us we could overcome the discomfort of uncertainty and be the change we needed to be.**

CHANGE IS UNCOMFORTABLE AND A CONSTANT STRUGGLE.

Jamar got us to realize that the most important people in making change were us. The most important person in championing Design Thinking in your organization is you. It's not your boss or the executives or even the person in charge of <u>change management</u>. It's you! The Design Thinking champion. As Gandhi said, "Be the change you want to see in the world."

If you want others to risk trying something new, then you must take risks too. If you want others to have confidence in you, then you must have confidence in yourself. Championing Design Thinking takes courage, confidence, and persistence.

BEING PASSIONATE ABOUT DESIGN THINKING IS NOT ENOUGH.

Championing Design Thinking requires effort—a persistent struggle against powerful forces. Don't just bemoan this struggle, embrace it. Be even more passionate about the champion's struggle than you are about Design Thinking itself. (You already are because you are reading this book!)

EMBRACE THE CHAMPION'S STRUGGLE?

Relish the challenge, use your curiosity, empathy building, and experimentation skills to overcome obstacles. This requires a big heap of persistence and a dab of flexibility. Jim Rohn, an entrepreneur and motivational speaker says, "If you really want to do something, you'll find a way. If you don't, you'll find an excuse."

Thriving in uncertainty takes initiative and resiliency. You must be enterprising and inventive when faced with it. This requires the passion to take what you're handed and make the most of it. Make your motto **"I Can Figure it Out"** or **ICFIO**. Championing Design Thinking is as much about attitude and perspective as it is about capability. Post the ICFIO motto. Keep it in view as a constant reminder of a champion's instinctive response to challenges.

Championing Design Thinking is a struggle requiring you to try new things. Trying new things can be thrilling and daunting at the same time. You feel excited and optimistic and nervous and unsure. Questions run through your head: Will it work? Will I look stupid? Can I do this? Who am I to try? Acknowledge that these thoughts and feelings are normal. They mean you are trying something new. That you are moving towards your goal. Make those questions visible by listing them on a **My Brain on New** diagram. Refer to it often. When you find yourself thinking those thoughts, you're on the right track!

Get intentional on where you apply your efforts in the struggle. Make an **Influence Bullseye Diagram**. In the inner circle write all the things that are in your control, in the middle ring write things you can influence, and in the outer ring things that are near impossible for you to control and influence. The number of things that are in your control and influence will surprise you. Focus on leveraging those in your efforts. Don't spend your time on things in the outer ring—they're just a waste of your energy.

 **CHAMPIONING DESIGN THINKING MEANS EMBRACING RISK.**

Having courage means to act on one's beliefs despite danger. As a champion, you face many dangers in your organization; the biggest is failure. What if the customer <u>interviews</u> don't yield new insights? Will our project lose its funding? What will others think of me? Will it ruin my chances for a promotion? Will I lose my job? Failure can have consequences. As a champion, you must be clear about your relationship with failure.

Design Thinkers try things before we know we have the right idea. Sometimes it works and sometimes it doesn't. When it doesn't, when it is a "failure", you learn something important that can improve your idea. You know the value of failure, but what failure are you willing to risk in championing Design Thinking in your organization?

HMW... **GET CLEAR ON OUR RELATIONSHIP WITH FAILURE?**

For any action, you need to ask yourself: What is the danger in this? What am I willing to risk? Should I play this one safe, risking only the loss of a little of my time, or place a big bet risking the loss of my job or something else in between? Deciding how much you are willing to risk is a personal call. But remember, we humans fear loss twice as much as gain. Champions face the danger of failure head-on. They take risks that exceed their comfort level. Be courageous. Be confident.

Explore your failure tolerance. Create a **<u>Risk/Reward Chart</u>** for a set of actions you are considering. You must decide what the scale of the axes should be. Is it the amount of energy you put in or the political capital you're willing to spend versus the level of engagement you will obtain or the amount of support you will gain? Then thoughtfully plot the actions you are considering on the graph. Step back and reflect on the relative risk and reward of each action. Is it worth the risk? What might the reward be? Remember, champions take bold actions in the face of uncertainty and risk. Then decide and go! (or not).

Failure and success are not opposites. Thomas J. Watson Sr., founder of IBM, said success is found on the far side of failure. Success comes from learning from a failure and imagining what you could do differently next time. Entrepreneurs call this the <u>pivot</u>. Create a **Pivot Plan**; record a failure you just had, what you learned from it, and list things you might try next. Reflect on these, then decide on how you want to proceed. Turn the failure into another way forward while always keeping your eye on the goal.

Get inspired by the failures of others. Which of your favorite authors were repeatedly rejected? Which athlete didn't make the team on the first tryout? Which entrepreneur didn't succeed on their first attempt? Study how they bounced back, the attitudes and skills they used. See what you can learn from their experience. Better still, attend a **<u>Fuckup Night</u>** and hear three to four people share their professional failures. Fuckup Nights' motto is "We Live Life Without Filters by Sharing Stories of Failure".

 **SHOWING CONFIDENCE BUILDS OTHER'S CONFIDENCE.**

If you think about it, experts exude confidence. People want to work with them and will follow their lead. As a champion you need to know your subject, speak with conviction, and believe in yourself. Champions need to show the confidence of an expert. Feeling unsure or being modest results in uncertainty in others and erodes their trust in you. But how can you exude confidence when you are uncertain?

HMW... **GIVE OURSELVES 100% PERMISSION TO BE THE EXPERT?**

Simple answer: give yourself 100% permission to be the expert, then fake it until you make it! Stay confident in the face of challenges; maintain the poise and conviction of an expert. (Warning — be careful not to cross the line from confidence into arrogance.)

THOUGHTS?

_____

_____

_____

_____

_____

_____

_____

_____

_____

_____

Build your confidence in your own expertise. You probably have more than you acknowledge; we are not always good at seeing our expertise for ourselves. So do an **Expert Interview:** pretend you are the eagerly awaited Design Thinking expert being interviewed on a popular podcast. Get one of your colleagues to play the host. Have them ask you probing questions to uncover the depth of your expertise. Record the interview. Play it back. Listen carefully. Based on what you hear, write a biography that highlights the depth of your expertise. Keep it handy and refer to it whenever you feel you're faking it.

Experience builds expertise and confidence. Is your current role keeping you from gaining experience you feel you need? Then consider a **Side Hustle**. Do a Design Thinking project outside of work. There are lots of organizations out there that need the skills of Design Thinkers; minor sports leagues, civil service groups, schools, local governments. Find one that interests you and volunteer to do a project for them. Use it as an opportunity to build your expertise and confidence. Plus, it'll make a brilliant case study of the power of Design Thinking.

There are plenty of schools around the world where you can get degrees in Design Thinking. All the leading business schools offer courses. But lots of people discover Design Thinking after developing expertise in other areas. They find it intriguing; a creative, freeing way to work. They put in the additional time and effort to become a Design Thinker. Maybe you are one of those people. While you have expertise in other areas, you feel you are a capable Design Thinker. But people don't view you that way. They value you for your other expertise. How can you show them that you are a Design Thinker? Get certified. Take a program from a reputable firm like the LUMA Institute. Let that attest to your Design Thinking expertise. **Get a Badge** that says you're an expert. Wear it proudly as a reminder to you and others.

 **CHAMPIONING DESIGN THINKING IS A MARATHON, NOT A SPRINT.**

"Man, this is hard!" "Oh, that didn't work." "Will I ever be able to get something to work?"
Along the way there will be dead ends, hurdles, and periods when it feels like you aren't making progress. You must stay determined and consistently show up day after day. But what can you do to keep your endurance up? What can you do to fuel your persistence?

HMW... FUEL OUR PERSISTENCE?

Keep a positive attitude even in difficult situations. Stay focused on actions you can take to move towards your goal. And stay away from negative thoughts. They can distract you and erode your persistence.

WHAT ARE YOU THINKING?

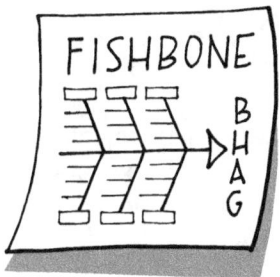

Getting your organization to embrace Design Thinking is a <u>BHAG</u> (Big Hairy Audacious Goal): a long-term goal that changes the very nature of a business. Breaking its enormity down into small actions can fuel your persistence. Instead of giving into feeling overwhelmed, focus on what you can do next. Create a **BHAG <u>Fishbone Diagram</u>**. Your BHAG is the head. Each of the bones are broad areas you want to focus on. Along each bone write actions you are considering for that area. Now you can be confident knowing that the actions you take will move you closer to your BHAG.

Sometimes it seems like you're not making progress. It feels like you're putting in a lot of effort with little to show for it. This makes it hard to keep up the positive attitude. As I have said, championing Design Thinking is a marathon, not a sprint. Often it's hard for you to recognize the distance you have covered. Develop the habit of writing a **What I Accomplished This Month Report**. Take a few minutes each month, reflect on the actions you have taken. Identify all the success you've had, no matter how small. Write a report to yourself. It's motivating to keep a running inventory of your accomplishments.

Small wins give you a boost. They are even more important than the occasional big win for keeping you motivated and creative. Don't miss the opportunity to pause and **Celebrate Small Wins**. Why not feel good about them? Why not be proud of what you have done? This can help you want to achieve even more. Celebrate in your own way. Share it with a friend. Take an espresso break. Go for a walk. Cheer out loud. Buy a new stack of sticky notes! Whatever reward makes you happy and enthusiastic. Make it a habit to celebrate small wins. Do it in the moment or at the end of each week.

 ## REJECTION IS AN OPPORTUNITY TO GET CURIOUS.

"I keep telling them it'll work. But why won't they listen to me?" There will be rejection and criticism. And it can feel personal. As any good salesperson will tell you, approximately 80% of people will reject a sales proposal four times before accepting it. Their rejection is not about you. They may need more time or more information.

HMW... NOT TAKE IT PERSONALLY?

So, no need to take rejection or criticism personally. Get curious instead, really curious. Get to the why of their opposition, then try a fresh approach to addressing it.

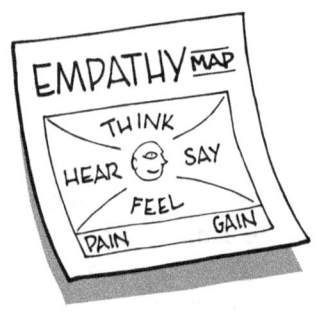

People can be stubborn and unreasonable when faced with the unfamiliar. It can feel like an emotional overreaction. But they are reacting based on their current understanding and past experiences. Instead of trying to convince them, take time to uncover the why of their resistance. Use your Design Thinking skills of interviewing and observation to discover what is driving their behavior. Capture your findings on an **Empathy Map**. Look for insights in what you have learned. Pay close attention to their current pains and desired gains. Then develop an approach for convincing them grounded in their perspective.

When people are critical or judgmental, it's not about you. It can be about their needs, their fears, their desire for control. And it is also about YOU. Hearing negative comments can feel personal; it can trigger an emotional reaction from you. And emotional reactions aren't always the most constructive. They often happen quickly, without consideration on your part. The trick to avoiding emotional reactions is to name your <u>triggers</u> and recognize when someone has pulled them. Make a **Triggers List**. Think of times when you have had an emotional reaction. What was it that triggered you? Not being respected? Being treated unfairly? Being misunderstood? Watch for your triggers. Notice when they are about to be pulled. Then pause. Now you can respond constructively without taking it personally.

Negative feedback can feel personal if you don't view it simply as information. Think of a <u>design critique</u>, a session where you get constructive feedback on your <u>concept</u>. People give you positive and negative feedback. As the presenter, your role is to harvest as much of it as possible. It is not to defend your concept or sell your idea. It is to learn as much as you can to improve your concept. Ultimately, you get to decide what feedback you will use in the next iteration of your concept. Why not adopt a **Critique Mindset** when faced with feedback that feels personal? Ask yourself what is the information behind what they are saying? What is the real reason they are saying this? How could that inform my next steps? You get to decide what is valuable for your purposes and leave the rest behind.

NEWS

TAKE #17

LANGUAGE

VALUES

MEDIUM

MESSAGE

THESAURUS

SO WHAT?

"They just don't get what we do!" "They don't understand us and we don't understand them." "Never put me on another project with this client!"

This is what we were hearing from our teams as they struggled to work with one of the world's largest consumer goods company. And we had to do something about it. And fast.

The client was renowned for its data-driven processes, science-based R&D, and risk averse culture. Design Thinking was unfamiliar to them at the time. On top of that, they had their very own language of made-up corporate speak, arcane technical terms and hundreds of acronyms. As Design Thinkers, we were experiencing both a clash of cultures and a dash of lost-in-translation. "This is like <u>statistical regression analysis</u> meets <u>thumbnail sketching</u>," I thought.

We needed to overcome the lost-in-translation problem. So, we created an extensive glossary of terms – terms they used and terms we used. We shared the glossary with everyone on both sides. We discovered several words had very different meanings for each side. For example, "concept" meant an early fuzzy idea worthy of further exploration to us. For them it meant a well-defined product idea derived from research ready for large-scale consumer testing! Frustration? No wonder!

To help them better understand our approach, we needed to communicate in their language, scientific sounding language. Instead of, "Let's do some <u>clustering</u> with sticky notes," we would say, "Let's do some pattern identification with a data set." Think about it. A brief phrase or quick sketch on a sticky note is a data point. A bunch of these sticky notes is a data set. A well-clustered bunch of sticky notes reveals patterns to consider. "Data", "data set" and "patterns in the data" used their vocabulary; "sticky notes" and "clustering" used ours.

We also recast how we described things so they spoke to the objective we were trying to achieve: making sense of the data. Who cared about clustering anyway? What was really important were the patterns clustering revealed. The meaning we extracted from them was what we were after; how we got there was secondary.

PEOPLE DISMISS WHAT I'M SAYING.

Have you ever started a new job in a new organization? Did you have trouble understanding what was being said? The abbreviations? The unfamiliar words? Did you feel like they were speaking another language? That's because people in organizations develop their own internal language. It serves as a kind of shorthand, an everyday way of reducing uncertainty and communicating efficiently. They base this language on "the way things are done around here."

PEOPLE WON'T EMBRACE WHAT THEY CAN'T UNDERSTAND.

When the language of an alternative way of doing things like Design Thinking appears, it takes effort for people to understand. It sounds fuzzy and often gets dismissed.

HMW... SPEAK IN THEIR LANGUAGE?

You know, making Design Thinking easy to understand increases the likelihood others will adopt it. That's why as a champion you need to speak in their language, not designer-ese.

Design Thinking has a language of its own. To others it's jargon, lots of fluffy words – not serious business. But you know it is. So, make it sound serious. Create a Design Thinking Translator for you to use. For each Design Thinking concept or method, create a definition that uses the language of your organization. Maybe "fail fast fail often" becomes "run a series of experiments" or "envisioning" becomes "generating strategic alternatives." Create a **Design Thinking Translator** and use it!

Is your organization an Agile organization? Does it use <u>Business Model Canvases</u> or <u>Six Sigma</u>? Every organization has processes for getting work done. Design Thinking has its own process. But we can apply most Design Thinking methods inside of the others. Agile uses a set of customer requirements. Business Model Canvases use value propositions. Six Sigma uses team collaboration. These are all outputs that Design Thinking produces. Create a **Design Thinking Thesaurus**. Identify the key processes in your organization, the major phases, the steps used, and the outputs produced. Then map Design Thinking methods against them. Now instead of saying "Let's try Design Thinking" you can say "I have an interesting way to do our next <u>Agile sprint retrospective</u>."

"How are you today?"– "Not bad" vs "How are you today?" – "Great!" Which exchange feels better? Which one would give you a positive impression? The language you use affects how others receive your message. **Positive language** can reduce people's defensiveness and increase their optimism. It can increase your credibility. Using the future tense is also powerfully positive: "Imagine when we succeed" or "You'll look forward to trying it." Resist the temptation to slip into negative language when things get tough. Stay on the positive side of language.

TEDx speakers make presenting look effortless. While their topics may differ, they have one thing in common. They rehearse their presentations repeatedly in front of others. Rehearsing a presentation grows your confidence and allows you to refine your message. Do you have an important one coming up? **Rehearse it** with a colleague. Have them <u>role play</u> your intended audience. Then ask them for specific feedback on your material. Are my major points clear? Am I using the right language? Is my message convincing? Then refine your presentation and try again. Practice may not make perfect, but it sure can make it better. As a Design Thinker, you know the power of iteration.

 **PEOPLE LISTEN FOR WHAT IS IMPORTANT TO THEM.**

Internal language expresses the culture of an organization. Everything from the mission statement down to taboo words are expressions of what is valued and what isn't. Company mottos like "Just get 'er done!" "The customer is always right!" "Safety first" are powerful indicators of what is valued.

HMW... MAKE WORDS THAT MATTER?

Communicate in ways that show Design Thinking is aligned with those values. How can it lead to strong action or elevate the customer or lower the risk of harm? Show Design Thinking is consistent with people's values by using words that matter.

An organization's values are the principles and beliefs that guide people in achieving its goals. Some organizations value efficiency, others value serving their communities, others the triple bottom line. People are more likely to listen and consider novel approaches if they align with these values. Do a **Values Audit** of your organization. Identify what is most important to people. Listen to the language they use. Determine the basis for their decision making. See what gets rewarded (or not!) Watch how they do their work. Pay attention to what the leaders say and do. This will help you uncover your organization's values. Then write them down. Refer to them often. Be sure to speak to what is really valued.

Design Thinkers have a bias to action. We are doers, excited to apply Design Thinking methods. We talk about how important it is to have empathy. How doing interviews with <u>extreme users</u> or <u>walk-a-mile immersions</u> helps us do that. This is all well and good. However, others are most interested in results: tangible, observable results. That's why it's important to frame your communication in terms of the **So What?** Your messaging should emphasize the results first. Then describe how you can get the desired result through the Design Thinking approach. Instead of saying, "We can use interviews and observations to build empathy with our customers." Try "We will define our value proposition through a deep understanding of our customer's needs. I have a couple ways we can do that." The value proposition is the result, the most important thing. The interviews and <u>observations</u> are secondary. Put the "So What?" first.

Marshall McLuhan, the Canadian communication theorist, said, "<u>The Medium is the Message.</u>" He asserted that the form of the message determines the way others will perceive it. We all have ways we prefer to send and receive information. Email or chat, in-person or via video. As a champion, understand what medium your audience prefers. First, who is the audience? Senior leadership? People in another department? A key individual whose support you need? Understand how they like to get information. Do they like dense Word docs or high-level summaries, videos of actual customers or a graph of customer survey feedback? The medium is also the kind of information that is most convincing for them. Facts and figures? Expert opinions? Past successes? Knowing their preferred medium allows you to tailor your message to get the biggest bang for your buck.

Design Thinking champions are spokespeople for the cause. Have you noticed great spokespeople compress their messages into pithy quotes or headlines? **Headlines** are short, impactful, relevant and memorable. When you don't have time to tell a full story, start with the punchline. Think Twitter, tag lines, elevator pitches. Capture your listener with the primary message first. Start with it. Repeat it throughout the conversation. And most importantly, end with it. Be sure it is the one thing they remember. Make your headline only one or two lines. Use simple language, including power words – words that trigger an emotional response from the listener. Words that matter to them. Words that encourage them to take action and support you.

INQUIRE BEFORE CONVINCE

✓ INTERESTS
⊘ POSITIONS

UUU OF RESISTANCE

LOYAL SKEPTIC

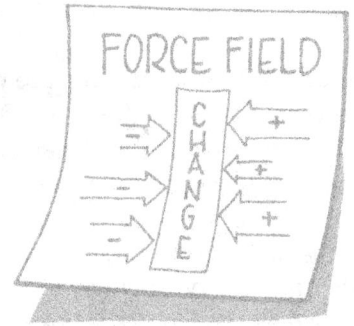

FORCE FIELD
CHANGE

OVERCOME A HURDLE

"IT'S NOT THE HORSE YOU'RE RIDING. IT'S HOW YOU ARE RIDING IT."

Ted stood up and stormed out of the conference room. He'd had enough of arguing with me in front of the VP and the rest of us managers. I had been trying to get him to relinquish some control over the approval of changes to production processes in our manufacturing plants. I was tired of hearing the plant engineers complain that, "You corporate types take forever to approve changes." Timely approval would speed up the time to market for the new products we were designing. In their eyes Ted, Manager of Corporate Engineering, and his team were the problem. The answer seemed so clear to me: give the plant engineers the authority to approve changes. They were qualified engineers, as was Ted and his team. I was trying to get Ted to see it as clearly as I did. And clearly, I hadn't. I was stumped. The conference room emptied, leaving only me and the VP.

"Samir," I said, "am I not right?" He looked up at me and said, "Dan, it's not the horse you're riding it's how you are riding it." I thought for a few minutes, got up and walked back to my office. "Hmm", I thought. "It's not the horse, it's how I was riding it? Guess I must find another way to ride."

Confronting Ted with *my* solution in our meeting wasn't the best way to *ride*. First, I needed to speak with Ted and apologize, then try to understand why he was so opposed to letting the plant engineers approve changes. Why was my solution not the right one in his mind?

I went to Ted's office, sat down and apologized for my actions in the meeting. He told me how frustrated he was with the whole situation (and with me). How he and his staff were working their butts off, but the backlog of change requests wasn't getting any smaller. How his request to hire more staff had just been turned down.

As I listened, it still puzzled me why he didn't like *my* solution. I asked. His answer surprised me. Outside agencies certified all our products to be safe for consumers. Ted and his team were responsible for ensuring they complied with their standards. Changes to our production processes could jeopardize that certification and, even more concerning, the safety of our products for consumers. No wonder he was so reticent "to give up control." I now understood why he was resisting *my* solution.

In the spirit of staying with the same horse, just riding it differently, I decided to see if I could get Ted to consider letting the plant engineers approve changes. How could it help Ted and his staff reduce their workload while ensuring the products remained certified and safe for consumers? After a few lively discussions and some analysis, we realized most production changes the plant engineers were requesting did not affect certification or safety. Approving those changes could be their responsibility. Changes that could affect certification and safety would remain the responsibility of Ted's team. By "riding my horse differently," I made *my* solution for getting our new products to market faster Ted's solution for reducing his team's overload.

 ## PEOPLE DON'T SEE IT MY WAY.

As a champion, you believe Design Thinking is just what your organization needs.
But when you share your enthusiasm with others, you face resistance. So, you try even harder and face even stronger resistance. It's maddening.

 ## THERE ARE REASONS WHY THEY'RE RESISTING.

Uncovering the reasons driving people's resistance is key to overcoming it. You must take the time to use your powers of inquiry to understand their perspective and empathize with their situation.

HMW... MEET THEM WHERE THEY ARE?

What are they trying to achieve? What is holding them back? Based on this understanding, find ways that work for them. Then you can make what you want, what they want. Make Design Thinking the solution to their problem.

As a champion, you work publicly to build support for Design Thinking. You are an advocate. Advocates develop good relationships. They use their strong communication skills. They stand up and challenge decisions. But most importantly, they develop a deep understanding of the opposing view. Success as an advocate begins with listening to the reasons for resistance. Our tendency is to jump to the convincing part of advocacy, eloquently espousing the virtues of Design Thinking. This can get you into trouble. If resisters don't feel you understand them and take them seriously, they will dig their heels in even deeper. Get curious and put your Design Thinking interviewing skills to work. Ask them for concrete information. Don't agree or disagree. Build empathy for their situation. Ask what and how questions. Why questions can cause defensiveness. Provide straightforward and honest answers to their questions. Remember: **Inquire Before Convince**. Listening closely to resistance provides you with the information to be convincing.

People's resistance to trying alternative approaches comes in many forms — defensiveness, apathy, stonewalling to name a few. This is tiring for a champion like you. But these are only symptoms of the genuine reasons for their resistance. They are either **Unaware, Unwilling, Unable** – the 3 big reasons for resistance. If they are unaware, they don't have the knowledge of Design Thinking or its potential. You will need to spark their curiosity. Help them learn why it will work for them. If they are unwilling, they are not yet committed to it. You will need to uncover the why of their unwillingness by listening with empathy. If they are unable, they just can't do it. You will need to encourage and assist them in acting. Getting clear about the "U" you're facing will help you tailor your efforts and get them on board.

They are always asking troublesome questions. Doubting the answers you give. Ever reluctant to shift their beliefs despite your efforts. A skeptic is just plain infuriating. But they can become your best ally if you turn them into a **Loyal Skeptic**. To convert a skeptic into a Loyal Skeptic, you must filter out the personal, unproductive parts of their criticism and find what is relevant and useful. What is the basis of their reluctance? Acknowledge the shortcomings of your idea. Ask them what they would do if they were you. Let them put it in their words. Give them credit for their ideas, even if they are yours. Include them on your team. Allow them to ask the hard questions. This increases their certainty and confidence. It also builds their trust in you. Once they feel involved in something they wanted no part of, they become a Loyal Skeptic. Then use them as powerful advocates to make other skeptics believers too.

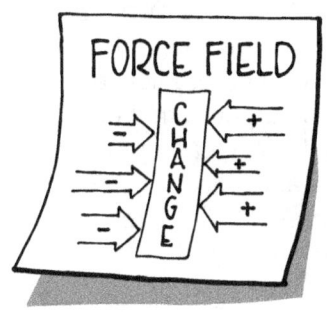

There are many forces acting on people in organizations. External forces such as project deadlines, reporting requirements, budget constraints. And internal forces such as a desire for status, a sense of accomplishment, feeling part of something bigger than themselves. Negative forces play into people's resistance to try alternative approaches like Design Thinking. Positive forces can move them closer to adoption. Explore the many facets of their resistance by plotting the forces acting on them on a **Force Field Map**. This will help you find opportunities to strengthen the forces that support your efforts and weaken the ones that don't. Start by writing in the center of the map the change you want: their support for a cool project, money in next year's budget. Then describe the forces acting on them: their pros and cons, their actions and reactions, their ideal situation and their reality. Draw arrows for each force using their length to indicate their strength. Based on the mapping, identify actions you can take to increase the positive forces and minimize the negative forces acting on them. Let the forces be with you!

Sometimes meeting someone where they are means meeting them where they are stuck. They could be struggling to **Overcome a Hurdle**. Because of this, they don't have the time or energy to even consider Design Thinking. Helping them overcome a hurdle is an opportunity for you to show the results Design Thinking can produce. A chance to build their trust in you and become a valuable ally. Identify a major hurdle they are facing and work a Design Thinking method with them to overcome it. Maybe it is prioritizing next year's projects at planning time. Facilitate an <u>Importance Difficulty Matrix</u> with them. Maybe it's dealing with a disagreement over the best feature set. Work a <u>Bullseye Diagram</u> with them. Get creative and get them over their hurdle. They will appreciate it.

You want to take the fastest route to your destination. Your fellow traveler wants to take the slower but more scenic route. You both have an interest in getting to the destination. But you have differing positions on how to get there. What do you do? Do you take the fastest route on the way there and the scenic route on the way home? Or maybe you alternate the fastest and the scenic routes throughout the trip? Or maybe you just agree to meet there and go separately! People take positions, fast or scenic, they believe best address their interests – getting to the destination. To meet someone where they are, look past their position to their underlying interest. **Interests vs Positions**. Don't argue with their position of "Our current ideation process works just fine." Get them to acknowledge what their actual interest is: a lot of creative ideas. Then work with them to explore other, better ways to address their interest. Maybe using a <u>Creative Matrix </u>instead of <u>Brainstorming</u>!

"Our innovation system isn't working. All we are getting is small incremental ideas from our officers. We need something different." After a few minutes of discussion with Chen, I could see why. The civil service had spent a fortune on idea bank software, then required each of their officers to enter at least 2 ideas per month. They now had a vast repository of ideas ranging from switching from fluorescent to LED lighting in the hallways to new noodle dishes for the cafeteria menus! It was essentially a mandatory digital suggestion box. It discouraged Chen. He wanted big ideas – ideas that would revolutionize the way the government provides services to its citizens. He wasn't getting them.

"We have invested so much money and effort over the last few years, but we are still not getting results. Even though our leaders know this, I can't get support for trying something else. I'm stuck." He needed help. He had to build support toward a new way of innovating.

So, we hatched a plan. Chen would get the leaders of a few government ministries to identify a vexing problem they were facing. Then we would work with a small team from each of those ministries and use Design Thinking to come up with innovative solutions. We'd be taking a big risk as no one on the teams had used Design Thinking. Vexing problems and inexperienced teams be damned! Chen was willing to take the risk. We'd make it work and show that Design Thinking can produce the big ideas he was looking for.

One team was from the Ministry of Revenue, the dreaded tax collectors. Their vexing problem? Reducing the time officers spent dealing with delinquent taxpayers. They were looking for better ways of enforcing the regulations for filing and paying taxes.

Just the thought of interviewing delinquent taxpayers was scary for the team. They just couldn't imagine, "Hello I'm from the Ministry of Revenue and I'm here to do some ethnographic research on your non-payment of taxes." Yet they embraced the challenge and good thing they did. They discovered the two types of people who made up most of the delinquent taxpayers. The first group were young professionals who had just begun their careers. They didn't realize they needed to file an annual tax return. "Taxes are being taken out of my paychecks every week. Why do I need to file?" The second group, disorganized people, were just plain old scatterbrains. "Oh, there is a filing deadline? When was that?"

41

Aha! The Ministry of Revenue didn't have an enforcement problem, it had an education and communication problem. The team presented this reframing to their leaders along with a set of creative solutions. Several got approved and implemented. It was now apparent to the leaders that Design Thinking produced bigger, more innovative ideas than anything ever submitted to the idea bank. Chen got the support he needed and went on to roll out Design Thinking government wide.

 ## PEOPLE WANT PROOF.

Success gets people's attention. Showcasing results is a powerful strategy for getting people to take up Design Thinking. Create a success and make sure others know about it. It builds their confidence and support.

 ## NOTHING IS MORE CONVINCING THAN SUCCESS.

First, be clear on how your organization defines success. What do people in your organization really care about? Is it speed to market? Customer satisfaction? Collaboration across departments? Progress towards a lofty mission?

HMW... MAKE SUCCESS SPEAK FOR ITSELF?

Show how Design Thinking can deliver results. While success can speak for itself, it often needs help. So, find creative and compelling ways to make it visible to as many people as you can.

After buying the latest gadget, have you watched a YouTube demonstration video to figure out how to make it work? Demos allow you to learn for yourself. Doing a Design Thinking **Demo** can give people a low-risk way to build their understanding and confidence before adopting it. A place where they can experience getting results. Do a small scale but high-profile project. Enroll key stakeholders onto the project team. Limit the project scope to lower their perceived risk. Maybe it's developing a new process within your department. Or working with a willing client to better understand their customers. Or understanding the unmet needs of colleagues working from home. Then work your Design Thinking magic with them. Remember the proof will be in (the making of) the pudding!

Sometimes it's difficult to show a big success. Maybe you don't have the mandate or resources. You lack the opportunity to show a big Design Thinking win. No worries. Small wins can be just as convincing as big ones. A series of small achievements can also help you put the power of Design Thinking on display. Making them visible can attract allies and win over resisters. They also build your confidence and gain support for going after even bigger wins. Select a series of small but significant tasks that others will watch with interest. Apply your Design Thinking skills. Show some wins. Be a champion by making a **Mountain from Molehills**.

Professors use them to challenge students' thinking. Marketers use them to get customers to take action. Business people read them to remain up to date. Harvard Business Review has made a business out of them. Case studies are a powerful tool for champions. They are real-life stories with an air of authority. You can find lots of Design Thinking case studies. But the most convincing are ones that detail a success within your own organization. They make it nearly impossible for anyone to say, "That won't work in our organization" because it did! So, **Make a Case** by writing a case study. Find an example of a successful application of Design Thinking in your organization. Maybe in another department, office or division. If you can't find one, make one yourself by doing a project. Then write and share the case study. A well-written case study makes the business case that Design Thinking can succeed in your organization.

Being recognized by unbiased experts can boost your credibility. Think "Oscar Bump" for an actress or a Zagat 5-star rating for a restaurant or the World Cup for a soccer team. Awards are reputation builders. They raise your visibility and attract attention. They can be a testament to your Design Thinking capabilities and build others' confidence in you. Go win an award! Maybe it's a design award for a project you are proud of or an industry award for the success you've had using Design Thinking. Or maybe it's the associate of the year award for achieving an important organizational goal using Design Thinking. Then share the news. Add it to your email signature and online profiles. Even if you end up as a runner-up, preparing the award submission forces you to clearly communicate the impact you had using Design Thinking. Use the information to create a compelling case study. **Give Yourself a Bump** and show others what it took to win and what success can look like.

Seeing someone else succeed can be a huge motivating factor, especially if it's your competitor! Competing allows us to satisfy our need to win. It challenges us to improve our performance. We learn from our competitors as we watch them advance. And it doesn't feel good to be behind. You can use competition to motivate others to consider Design Thinking. Find examples of competitors using it to move ahead of your organization. Watch for their success stories in industry association news, online Design Thinking groups, competitor's blogs, business or design school case studies. Then use creative ways to share them broadly within your organization. George Steinbrenner said, "Second place is really the **First Loser**." No one wants to be a loser. Especially people in your organization.

To paraphrase Dr. Howard Gardner, "Stories constitute the single most powerful weapon in a *champion's* arsenal." People learn vicariously and discover lessons for themselves when listening to an engaging story. It puts them in the context and helps them to understand the situation. They feel a part of it, especially if it taps into their emotions. That's what makes stories memorable. But as a Design Thinker, you know this. That's why you use storyboards to tell the story of a new service or role play for a new use scenario. Even if your organization likes spreadsheets and PowerPoint decks, don't forget the power of stories. Build a library of Design Thinking success stories. Stories that illustrate the points you want to make. Remember, engaging stories follow a journey: the hero is in an unsatisfying situation. She starts her quest then faces and overcomes challenges to arrive at a new better place. Use quotes and sound bites that people will remember. When faced with a challenge pull out a champion's favorite weapon: well-crafted success **Stories**.

SLIP INTO A STRUGGLE

DRAW ATTENTION

INFILTRATE TRIED & TRUE

MAKE IT EVERYDAY

GO IT ALONE

ENGAGE A HIGHER POWER

DT WALLPAPER

Getting a highly successful organization to adopt new practices to drive innovation is a classic challenge facing leaders like Tamika, the EVP of Innovation for one of the world's leading executive education organizations. Although it was an early innovator in the field, over the years the organization had become rigid and resistant to change. As a result, they were falling behind the times. Tamika's charge was to overcome this resistance and make the organization innovative again. Being a savvy leader, she tried making innovation an organization-wide strategic initiative. While her fellow executives expressed support, concrete actions like making the required investment never happened. Frustrated but ever the optimist, Tamika decided to take another approach.

"Dan, I have put together a small team to develop educational programs for underserved people in developing countries; people we currently don't reach. We need to deliver the programs for a fraction of the cost of our existing programs. And I mean for pennies a day per person, not the thousands of dollars per day we currently charge! We haven't been able to figure out how. Will you work with the team and use Design Thinking to crack this one?" **Tamika continued. "There is little support for this, so it can't be an official project. I have only a tiny budget but, I really need this to succeed. We need to show the organization what innovating looks like."**

Wicked challenge, little support, tiny budget, show how to innovate? Never one to shrink from an opportunity to use Design Thinking for good, I agreed to work with the team. And I knew the small group Tamika had assembled was passionate about helping the underserved and enthusiastic about trying Design Thinking. They were the right crew for the job and somehow, just somehow, we would make it happen.

In our first team meeting we put together our plan for the ethnographic research, prototyping and testing we would do when we immersed ourselves in far-away communities. We also discussed how we might showcase our use of Design Thinking to others in the organization. Of course, we would do updates on our little side project, but were there more subtle and informal ways? How could we showcase Design Thinking without being an official project? What might be more effective than a series of formal presentations?

We could not get a project room. We weren't an official project after all. Could we find some way to work in the midst of the organization? How about using the lounge just off the main hallway? That might work! Why not hold our working sessions there? We could post images from our research, <u>personas</u> we would develop, charts of our <u>sense making</u>; slowly exposing our progress and the new tools we were using to unsuspecting passersby. Why not give it a try?

Our first working sessions in the lounge attracted little attention other than a few snide comments like "How dare you use the lounge space for your project!" But as the weeks went by, people began to stop and listen in. Word spread and more people became curious about what we were up to. We knew we were onto something when people started attending our working sessions uninvited! They pulled up chairs and participated with us in the work. They were curious and asked probing questions. They were helpful and provided expertise. Our Design Thinking approach to our unofficial project was getting attention.

Then, one day, the unexpected happened. A statistician from the quantitative research department stopped me on her way to lunch. "Dan," she said, "you know the prototyping you and your team are doing? We've done nothing like that in our department. But a couple colleagues and I are trying it on one of our projects. We are very excited. I'll let you know how it goes."

Wow! People were taking our Design Thinking methods and trying them! It was becoming part of "how things are done around here." No formal strategic initiative needed. Taking the unfamiliar and making it familiar was working.

P.S. Tamika and her team achieved great things; their efforts resulted in the formation of an entirely new division of the organization. They developed and delivered education programs, helping hundreds of thousands of underserved people around the world. And it cost just pennies a day per person!

 PEOPLE WON'T EVEN TRY.

You can't get support to use Design Thinking on a "real" project. Why? Because people are uncomfortable trying unfamiliar ways of doing things. That's why making the unfamiliar familiar is a powerful tool for champions. A stealthy tool.

 IT'S EASIER FOR PEOPLE TO USE THE FAMILIAR THAN TRY THE UNFAMILIAR.

Exposing the elements of Design Thinking over time makes it easier for people to understand. And it allows them to try it before making a big commitment to use it on a full project.

HMW... BECOME THE FAMILIAR?

Infuse Design Thinking methods into everyday low risk activities. Don't make a big deal out of it. Just act like they are a natural way of doing things. Pretty soon people will build their own familiarity and willingness to use them.

We fill a working day in an organization with routine activities: staff meetings, Zoom working sessions, virtual coffee (or cocktail) hours. Working on a project team means remote collaboration, morning stand ups, after action reviews. Each of these represents an opportunity to use a Design Thinking method without needing official approval. Find such an opportunity. Select a suitable method and use it. Maybe Rose/Thorn/Bud at your weekly stand up. Others will see it in action. **Make it Everyday** so others get a chance to experience Design Thinking without making a big commitment.

There is always something teams struggle with, things they haven't figured out how to deal with yet. If you could find a way to help them solve their problem they'd breathe a collective sigh of relief. Maybe it's prioritizing an ever growing and shifting project list. Or getting alignment with another department on the scope of a joint project. Or communicating your findings to senior executives with short attention spans. Struggles abound in organizations. **Slip into a Struggle** the team is having by offering a Design Thinking method as an approach to overcoming it. "We've tried everything we can think of. What have we got to lose in trying this?" Then make it work! Getting a tangible result on a seemingly unrelenting struggle can work wonders for a champion.

SOP stands for <u>standard operating procedure</u>. A tried-and-true way of getting things done. Is your organization's SOP Agile, Stage Gate, <u>Voice of the Customer</u>, Six Sigma, or something else? Even for a champion like you, it is hard to get Design Thinking elevated to the level of a SOP right out of the box. Instead, try making it part of a system already in use. Collaborating efficiently, finding creative solutions, better serving the customer, getting results are things that SOPs seek to achieve. And they are all things Design Thinking can deliver. Find ways to insert Design Thinking methods into your organization's SOP. Don't make it about Design Thinking. Make it about making the SOP better. Show how it can deliver real results. **Infiltrate the Tried and True.**

Your organization has a strong culture based on an SOP. You are an Agile company, for instance. It's hard to even get an opportunity to try applying Design Thinking. How can you make it familiar if you can't even try it? Sometimes a champion needs to **Engage a Higher Power**. Someone who can require Design Thinking be used on a real project or initiative. Call in a favor from a more senior stakeholder. Ask them to be your sponsor and position Design Thinking as a build on the SOP. Have them set the expectation it will be used on the next project. Then get on with making it familiar.

A Design Thinker's ability to draw, draws people! The skill of painting a thousand words into a single picture fascinates them. How to illustrate complex concepts in simple ways. Thumbnail sketches, video clips, storyboards, or role plays stand in stark contrast to endless PowerPoint presentations and complex Excel spreadsheets. There are countless things communicated in organizations; the status of a project, the results of customer research, justification for investments, employee engagement levels, requests for funding. Use your Design Thinking skills and make every day communications engaging and compelling. People will notice. You will **Draw the Attention** of those who can help you champion Design Thinking.

You don't need anyone to come along with you if you Go it Alone. Demonstrate Design Thinking by using it on a project you are solely responsible for. Maybe it's the design of the department intranet site or creating a new employee onboarding policy, or finding the solution to a customer's problem. Choose a project that others are happy to have you do without them. Then rock it using your Design Thinking skills. The results will amaze them. They'll be curious about how you did it. Use a solo project to showcase the power of Design Thinking.

Have you ever redecorated a room in your apartment or house? After all the imagining, the choices and the work, you stand back and look. It seems all new and different. That is for about a week or two. Then it fades into normal again. It returns to being your familiar living space. Design Thinking can become familiar to others just by being in the environment. Use **Design Thinking Wallpaper**. Make evidence of Design Thinking visible to others wherever you can. Affinity clusters on a digital whiteboard as background for your video calls, personas of key customers in your monthly presentations, journey maps as the table of contents for your report. Find creative ways to infuse evidence of Design Thinking into the "environments" people in your organization inhabit.

"FIRST I'LL ASK HOW YOUR FAMILY IS DOING."

We weren't the most dysfunctional leadership team I had ever seen, but we were close. And Laura, our VP, had had enough. So, she gathered us for a weekend retreat. It was obvious we needed some remedial work. A casual dinner and cordial evening cocktails foreshadowed the tough conversations that were sure to happen the next day.

Kevin and I had a tough time working with each other. He ran the product management group with a firm hand. I struggled to convince him of the merits of the designs we created using Design Thinking. In my eyes, he was wrong for being so focused on low-risk line extensions over the riskier but potentially game-changing innovations we were developing. We weren't outright confrontational, but our discussions were getting more and more heated. I was hoping by participating in this retreat we could at least lower the temperature a bit.

Laura had planned the retreat for a few weeks. In preparation, we each had to complete a <u>self-assessment</u> (one of those where you rank your answers to a lot of weird questions). Laura was going to use them to make us aware of the differences in our personalities and communication styles that were fueling our dysfunction. I had never done a self-assessment before. I was not sure how it would help.

After breakfast the next morning, Laura laid out her expectations of us. The hard work needed for us to become a better leadership team was about to begin. Following a couple of team-building exercises, it was time to see the results of our assessments. Noor, the facilitator, passed out our reports. After a quick read through, we shared our individual results with each other.

Needless to say, Kevin and my profiles were quite different. He was an "Analytic" needing lots of facts before making decisions. Mine showed that I was a "Driver" boldly moving forward and focused on the big picture. He disliked small talk and wanted to get right to business. I preferred making a human connection before having a discussion. Interesting, I thought. So what? What would I do differently when I returned to the office? How would it help me work more constructively with Kevin?

The following Monday morning, I stood outside Kevin's office. I needed product management support for a development team I wanted to put together, support only Kevin could provide. Thinking about Kevin as the "Analytic" who needed facts and disliked small talk, I decided to have a different kind of conversation with him this time.

I knocked, entered his office and sat across the desk from him. Instead of asking how his family was doing, I got right to the reason for my visit. I needed product management support for a new development team.

"What information do you need to support this?" I asked. I spent the next half hour learning what data he was looking for. He asked for a lot. I knew I wouldn't be able to provide it all. But I realized I could find some to help him make the right decision.

Before I left his office he said, "Dan, this has been one of the best discussions we have ever had." He paused a minute and continued, "And, the next time I come to your office I'll start the conversation by asking how your family is doing."

After some work, I provided Kevin with the information I could find. He reviewed it and assigned a product manager to the team. Instead of trying to get him to see I was right, I flexed my approach. I responded to his need for facts. The team went on to design and successfully launch a whole new category of products.

_____

_____

_____

_____

_____

_____

_____

_____

 ## SOME PEOPLE ARE REALLY FRUSTRATING.

Because we are champions, when we meet resistance we try harder. We make our arguments more persuasive. We refine our logic to make it "irrefutable." We become more assertive because we know we are right. This forceful approach can lead to more intense push back from others.

 ## IT'S NOT WHAT'S RIGHT FOR YOU
THAT MATTERS MOST.

No one likes to be told over and over again they are wrong.

HMW... MAKE THEM RIGHT?

People want to feel like they are doing the right thing. Step away from the Us versus Them. Make Design Thinking right for them.

As a Design Thinker you know the power of the "yes and." Taking another's idea, acknowledging it and then building on it leads to better ideas. It's kind of like Judo (which means the gentle art in Japanese), the art of not resisting. Judo is about taking the other's force, adding to yours and using it to your advantage. When faced with resistance, don't fight back; use the gentle art. Instead of refuting their position, "yes and" them. Go back and forth with them. Build on their position. Move it closer to yours. Help them get themselves to being right about Design Thinking. Use **Yes And Judo**, a champion's move.

People who are resisting can seem unreasonable. You've been clear about why the time is right for Design Thinking. They just keep finding problems with it. You try to address their concerns with more rationale. They raise more problems. You feel you are in an endless loop of frustrating conversations. How do you break out? Sometimes it serves a champion to be humble. Acknowledge you don't have all the answers. Ask them for how they might address the problem. This lowers their defenses. It takes them from problem raising to problem solving. Engage them in co-creating a better idea with you. And surprise! It also can disrupt your thinking. Maybe there are things you hadn't yet considered that you should. Admit you don't have all the answers. Then work with them to find what's **Right - Right** for both of you.

As a champion, you deal with all kinds of people. Some you get along with. Some are just plain difficult to deal with. Some you communicate well with. Some you can't seem to get through to. You don't need to like everybody. But you do need the flexibility to effectively relate to them. We all have ways we like to be engaged. Knowing other's preferences and flexing your approach is a mark of a champion. But first you must know your own preferences. Just because you like to talk about the big ideas doesn't mean others do. Perhaps they want to hear about results, or they want data. That's where self-assessments like MBTI®, DiSC® and StrengthsFinder® come in. By completing a self-assessment, you can uncover your preferences. You can also learn the range of preferences others can have. Using this understanding, you can now flex your approach and make it right for them. **Assess and Flex**.

Are you working with someone who is trying Design Thinking for the first time? Maybe they were skeptical and reluctant to try. Yet you still got them past that point. The project is underway. They're trying their best but practicing Design Thinking is new and difficult for them. They're not sure if the project will be a success. You sense they have wondered, "Am I doing this right? Will I ever be able to do this Design Thinking thing?" Now's the time for a champion to make them right about what they are doing. Watch for specific things they are doing. Things that show they are in fact starting to build their Design Thinking muscles. As soon as you see it, let them know. Be sincere in your feedback. Deliver it in a way that's meaningful for them. Keep them on the **Right Track** by making them feel right.

She is the technical expert. The one who is going to do the detailed implementation of the solution the team is working to find. As the Design Thinker, you know the value of spending time in the Discover Phase, the value of insights that come from a deep understanding of the customer. She thinks all the time being spent on research is of little value. She is feeling the pressure of the timeline. She wants to start building the solution. The idea of cutting the discovery phase short irks you. This is where the double diamond model comes in handy. Use it to orient her. Build her confidence that there will be time for the implementation. Show her you are in the "getting to the right problem" diamond. The "getting to the right solution" diamond will follow. That's where she gets to be the star. Make her right about her concerns. The **Double Diamond is Your Best Friend**. Use it when others aren't feeling right about where they are with Design Thinking.

MAKE THE LINK

WALK A MILE

CAMEO APPEARANCE

GET UP CLOSE AND PERSONAL

PERSONA — MAKE THEM REAL

CHANNEL SOCRATES

After hearing our presentation, reviewing the prototypes and scrutinizing our business plan, Anna our CEO said, "I'm not sure…" My heart dropped. Our team had been working on the design of the new product line for months. After extensive research, design, and testing, we were sure we had a winner. We now needed the approval from the executives for the investment required to take them to market. But Anna obviously had some reservations. My mind darted back over all the details of the business plan, the results of the consumer testing, the pricing studies — all the hard work we had done. What had we missed? What was Anna concerned about? Hadn't we covered all the bases?

I looked around the room. The other executives looked perplexed too, as they saw we had a strong business case. I watched my team go from enthusiastic to deflated. I had to ask. "What aren't you sure about, Anna?" She replied, "I don't like the designs." Not exactly what the head of design wants to hear from the CEO. But I was sure the design was right. I decided to be bold.

I said, "It's good to know you don't like the designs, but that really doesn't matter in this case." She gave me a puzzled look. I continued. "If the target customer was a high net-worth Italian-American senior executive, your dislike of the designs would carry some weight. But as we have said, our target customers have annual family household incomes of $50,000. They buy and install the products themselves, like Maria." I pointed to a life-size cutout of Maria we had brought into the room to personify the customers we were after.

Was that bold or had I just committed a career altering (or possibly ending) move? Anna paused and said, "You're right, Dan. The research shows the designs have tested well with the target customers." I breathed a sigh of relief. The executive team approved the investment and adjourned the meeting. As Anna was leaving the room she turned around, smiled and said, "I still don't like the designs, Dan."

 ## PEOPLE WITH POWER THINK THEY DECIDE.

As a champion of Design Thinking, you run into resistance. Sometimes from people with power. Their power can come from their position in the organization or the credibility they have with others or the facts and figures they wield.

 ## THE CUSTOMER ALWAYS HAS THE FINAL SAY.

There is a higher source of power – the customer. The people that buy your product or use your service or the citizens you serve or the other department you supply information to. Without customers, your organization would not survive for long. Even people with power listen carefully to what they say.

HMW... TAKE IT BACK TO THE CUSTOMER?

When you face resistance, the customer is a formidable ally. Show how Design Thinking can help you get to know the most important person in your organization. Take it back to the customer.

_____

_____

_____

_____

_____

_____

_____

"Our customers just want the highest quality at the lowest price." "Our customers in that region don't buy premium packages." "Our customers use our service because we are the market leader." People in organizations think they know their customers. But often it's a shallow understanding, more a set of unquestioned beliefs based on company lore than an in-depth understanding of their customers. This can pose lots of challenges for a Design Thinking champion. And lots of opportunities! Create personas of your customers and show a clear picture of their motivations, aspirations, and their problems. Show others how Design Thinking uncovers valuable customer insights to drive your organization's success – how Design Thinking can **Make Them Real.**

We live in the era of online collaboration, remote teams and Zoom fatigue. This reminds us of the power of face-to-face interactions with others. There is something about them that makes our interactions more personal, makes understanding others easier. People in organizations rarely have the chance to know their customers in this way. They base their understanding on reports of aggregated data from Marketing or the assertions of customer service reps. While these are useful, they can leave a lot open to interpretation. Your idea of what's important to the customer can differ from theirs. This can be an advantage for a Design Thinking champion. So, help others get up close and personal with your customers. Bring customers into your meetings and presentations, preferably in person, but via video will do. Allow others to get their questions answered by interacting with them. **Get Up Close and Personal**. Show how Design Thinking can uncover what really matters.

As a Design Thinker, you know the ultimate idea you present results from many iterations of prototypes and testing. The prototypes are based on an idea selected from a set of ideas generated in a brainstorming session. That selection is based on insights from the interviews and observations done with real users. The idea you are proposing is the last link in a chain of effort that began with a deep understanding of the user, your customer. That link may seem obvious to you, but it's not always obvious to others. A new and novel idea can seem arbitrary because others don't see it. **Make the Link** visible to others. Your pitch can build in chronological order from research to the final aha! moment. Or it can start with the big reveal, then show the supporting evidence. Either way, find creative ways to show how Design Thinking can make the link between your customers, a great idea, and your organization's success.

Native Americans say to truly understand someone you must first walk a mile in their shoes. Design Thinkers say being the customer is the ultimate empathy building method. **Walk a Mile Immersions** are a great way to get others to understand what's important to your customers and to experience the deep understanding of the customer that results from applying Design Thinking. If you're hitting resistance, take them on an immersion. Take them to your customer's workplace and have them do their job for a day. Have them try to use your software product in your customer's home office. Have them be the citizen and go through your onboarding process. A "walk a mile experience" will turn Design Thinking resisters into believers.

Have you ever watched a movie where a famous actor pops in unexpectedly? It catches your attention. It might make you laugh, but you can't help but notice. That's the power of a **Cameo Appearance.** When you know you're going to face resistance to an idea, prepare a customer cameo appearance – a short video clip that breaks the expected flow of your presentation or an audio recording played just at the right moment in a knockdown drag 'em out conference call. Show them how Design Thinking can bring the most powerful voice in your organization – the customer – into your decision-making.

Socrates, the founder of the western tradition of thought, said, "I cannot teach anybody anything. I can only make them think." Teachers who use his method don't provide students with direct answers to their questions. Instead, they offer questions to get them thinking for themselves. Switching from telling others to engaging their thinking works wonders for champions like you. When someone takes issue with your position or idea, **Channel Socrates**. Don't respond directly. Instead, ask a good question. Make them think. A great question to ask is, "What would the customer say?" Followed by "Why would they say that?" Followed by, "What ideas would you have?" then, "Why would the customer think those would be good ideas?" Get them to think through the customer's lens to learn the power of Design Thinking for themselves.

IDEAS?

WHO·DUN·IT?

HONEY

ATTRACTS...

MAX
70-20

1ST
ROUND PICK

YOURS
THEIRS

UNLOCKING

THE
GATEKEEPER

TOTALLY

RELATE

I was on my first stop of a multi-country trip. The CEO asked me to roll out the new product development process to all our offices. I worked for months developing the process (it included a heavy dose of Design Thinking) and I was excited to have the mandate to get it implemented. It was a critical component of our strategy to become the market leader. I had prepared extensive documentation and a kick-ass presentation. Most of all, I had a rock-solid rationale for why it made sense. I knew it would impress my colleagues, and they'd be eager to jump on board.

"Any questions or comments?" I asked as I finished up my presentation. "Seems clear. Thank you for the presentation, Dan." said Brett, the managing director of the office. As his staff was leaving the room, he looked at me and said, "Who are you to tell me how to run my office?" He turned around and left. It stunned me. After packing up my stuff, I left too.

While I was driving back to the airport, I did what the military calls an <u>after-action review</u> in my head. *What had I expected to happen?* Everyone in that office would no doubt see the value in the new process, how well thought out, why it made sense to use it and be eager to start. *What happened?* I did my presentation and then nothing. Nada. No engagement. And an outright rejection by Brett. *What would I do differently next time?* Hmm. I wasn't sure. But I knew there was no sense in continuing on my trip until I did. I changed my flight and flew home.

I spent the next few days pondering the situation. I had created a solid process, a needed process. I was sure of it. Yet, why wasn't it clear to my colleagues in that office? How could I get them to see what I saw? How could I get Brett and his staff on board? I had to find a way. Thinking back to my presentation I remembered some affirmative head nodding coming from Nasar, an engineer. He and I had a good working relationship. He was an up and comer that others respected. Unsure what to do next, I called him. Maybe he could help.

"Ya, Brett is kinda like that," Nasar said. "He doesn't like anyone messing around in his territory. Flying in and presenting the process as a given was probably not the best approach." "I see that now," I said. Nasar told me he believed the new process was a good one. Even if Brett couldn't see it, their office badly needed it. "What do I do?" I asked. "I'll work with you on making it happen here," he replied. And that is just what we did. Nasar had the knowledge of the operations and culture of the office, and I had the new process.

Over the next few months, Nasar and I ran some trials, starting under the radar. Our aim was to make the new process work in that office. Eventually we had some small successes using rapid prototyping and testing. We attracted the attention of the staff as they saw the potential to reduce rework they normally had to do after a new product launch. They started to engage with us. We had set things in motion.

During the next quarterly update at the corporate office, Nasar reported on the successes we were having and the potential others were seeing in the new process. Even though Brett was initially resistant, the executive team now saw his office as a shining example for the other offices to follow. He was leading the way in our effort to become the market leader. None of that would have happened if Nasar and I hadn't built an alliance of the willing.

WHAT
DO YOU
THINK?

_____

_____

_____

_____

_____

_____

_____

_____

_____

_____

_____

_____

BEING THE LONE VOICE ISN'T WORKING.

There's wisdom in the African proverb, "If you want to go fast, go alone. If you want to go far, go together." This rings true when Championing Design Thinking in an organization.

GOING IT ALONE WILL ONLY GET YOU SO FAR.

Countries, businesses and passionate individuals form alliances. They know the mutual benefit that comes from working together towards a common goal. They know 1+1=3. Align yourself with others and amplify each other's efforts.

HMW... BUILD ALLIANCES OF THE WILLING?

Look for people passionate about making your organization more creative, collaborative and customer focused. Respected people who have influence with others. People who take considered action. Collaborate with them. Leverage each other's expertise. Provide each other with feedback. Keep each other motivated. See how far you can go together.

When selecting allies go for the 1st round draft pick. Find the standout player who will build the strengths of your team. Be clear on the position you need them to play – the technical expert, the HQ perspective, the communications person. But the most important thing about an ally is who they are as a person. Here's what to look for: Personal motivation to achieve the goal. Willingness to listen. Strong social skills. Trusted by others. Cool under pressure. A growth mindset. Understands the intricacies of your organization. Sees the connections between the big picture and the details. Action taker. Wow, that's a lot! Of course, not even a **1st Round Pick** will have everything you are looking for. Pick the one that comes the closest and get on with the game.

There's lots to learn from reading books about championing change. It's even better to learn directly from someone who has done it. But the very best is to learn from someone who has done it in your own organization. Someone who has faced and overcome its unique challenges. Someone who has made it work. Find someone **Whodunit** in your organization. Maybe they drove the initiative to make Agile an accepted practice or changed people's mindset around diversity and inclusion or implemented a complex software system across the organization. Find a successful champion and learn from them. Seek their advice. Interview them. What worked? What didn't? Be bold and ask them to be your mentor. Ally with someone whodunit.

Being a champion means constantly trying things, learning from them and growing your capabilities. That's where the 70-20-10 rule comes into play. It says there are three types of experiences that help you learn and grow — 70% learning by doing, 20% learning from others, and 10% from training. A great place to maximize the 70 and 20 is a Community of Practice (CoP), a network of allies who help each other improve their practice. They learn from each other's successes and failures. They capture and share what works and what doesn't. They provide feedback and support to each other. Find a Design Thinking CoP or organizational change CoP. It could be inside your organization or outside of it. Join it and be an active participant. If you can't find one, start one! **Maximize the 70-20**.

Have you ever persuaded the maître d' to give you the table by the window or let you in, even though you didn't have a reservation? Then you know the power of **Unlocking the Gatekeeper**, someone who controls access to something you want. Gatekeepers can be a barrier to a champion's efforts. They can also be a key ally in getting resources and support you need. Maybe it's funding or technical expertise or the ear of a key decision maker. Knowing what you are looking for is the first step. The second is identifying the gatekeepers who can help you gain access. Create a Stakeholder Map. Map the people who control the resources you want. Map the relationships they have with others who can get you access. Pinpoint the key gatekeepers. Then work to make them your allies and unlock the resources you need.

Having trouble finding allies? Not sure if anyone is even interested? Potential allies could be anywhere, but you just don't know. If you can't find them, then attract them. Think of what draws people's attention. What's the honey of your organization? Is it Lunch and Learns with fancy pizza? Is it a guest speaker on an intriguing topic (like how cool Design Thinking is)? Is it contests with prizes? Is it being the first to discover a mind-bending podcast? Whatever it is, use it because **Honey Attracts** potential allies. See who shows up. See who expresses interest. See who comes for a second time. See who tells their colleagues about the "Design Thinking thing" they just attended. Discovering that person is a great starting point for nurturing a powerful ally.

A good ally shares your passion for the cause you both care about. Allies bring their expertise to reinforce yours in pursuit of that common goal. What if someone has expertise you need, but they don't share your passion? What can you do to make your passion their passion? Get them to experience the power of Design Thinking for themselves. Give them a visceral understanding to fuel their passion. Do it in ways that also builds their expertise. If they are in HR, do employee interviews with them. But do the interviews your way. Show them how a qualitative understanding is as valuable as the results from an employee engagement survey. If they code the website, spend a day-in-the-life of a user with them. Show how seeing it from the user perspective can help them prioritize the feature list for their next Agile sprint. Use Design Thinking to help build their expertise and **Make Your Passion Theirs**.

"Finally, somebody who really understands me! Somebody who really hears me. Somebody who can **Totally Relate**." We all know somebody like that. Somebody we can trust to help us because of our similar experiences. They make the best allies for a champion like you. There is a lot to learn from other Design Thinkers and champions. But learning from those who can totally relate to your situation is the best. So target those somebodies in the same industry. Or the ones with the same professional background. Or ones who hold similar positions in their organizations. Or ones who face the same resistance to Design Thinking as you do. Look for them in places like your UX community, or your local non-profit network, or your alumni association. Become allies with and learn from those who can totally relate.

HITCH A RIDE

TAKE IT TO TASK

GO FOR THE 3s

NURTURE A NEW NATURE

LAUNCH IN A SATELLITE

GO INFORMAL

Being responsible for our consulting firm's website, I could sympathize with Anita. Her organization's website needed a major overhaul – a huge undertaking, and a major investment for her non-profit. After some intense lobbying, she got approval to proceed. It was now a top priority for her marketing department and a strategic focus for the entire organization. But why the sympathy on my part? Anita was getting inundated with demands. Every department wanted their content on the landing page. Everyone had strong opinions on how the website should look and feel. I knew how loud and overwhelming those demands could get.

I also knew Jose, the CEO, had been struggling to shift the organization from an internal focus to a customer focus. He knew the new website needed to address the needs of the customers first. All those self-serving requests and opinions Anita was getting weren't helping. They needed a way to counteract them. Jose and Anita decided to use Design Thinking to redesign the site. That would put the customer first for sure. And maybe this project also could shift people's focus to the customer? Jose's previous efforts had yielded little results. But people were certainly paying attention to the website project.

Few people in the organization clearly understood the key customers. So, the first thing Anita's team did was to create customer personas. After analyzing customer data and doing ethnographic research, they arrived at four; Joseph, Julio, Janice and Bo. That turned out to be a good move. The team took large posters of the personas to their project updates. They used them to justify their design decisions and fend off unwanted self-serving suggestions. When challenged they would point to them and say, "Yes, but what would Joseph want?" Or "What information would Janice need to see?"

People paid close attention to the progress the team was making. Over time, the constant referral back to the personas helped people understand their key customers better. It surprised me when I saw copies of the personas posted on other department's bulletin boards. I was also hearing Joseph, Julio, Janice and Bo named in hallway and lunchtime conversations. The customer's voice was becoming part of the everyday conversations in the organization. Because everyone was paying attention to the website project, Jose's vision of a customer focused organization was being realized.

 ## PEOPLE AREN'T PAYING ATTENTION.

"What gets measured gets managed" so the management maxim goes. **People pay attention to what their organizations pay attention to.** That's the idea behind Key Performance Indicators (KPIs), the small set of measures that provide evidence you are making progress towards the organization's goals. KPIs focus your work and decision making. People pay attention to them because making their KPIs directly affects their pay and status.

 ## PEOPLE PAY ATTENTION TO WHAT THEY ARE FOCUSED ON.

Whether or not your organization uses KPIs, place Design Thinking in people's focus. Identify what people are paying attention to – their KPIs or increasing subscriptions or improving the quality of your service. Then work Design Thinking into those places.

HMW... BE IN THE FOCUS?

You don't even need to tell them it's Design Thinking. Just use the mindset and methods to help people achieve what they are focused on. They are paying attention. They'll see it work. They'll want more. Be in the focus of your organization.

Trying to get some traction using Design Thinking? Need a place to show its value? A place where others will notice? Then hitch a ride on an initiative that's important to your organization. Look for a project critical to achieving your organization's mission. One that is in your strategic plan. If there is no strategic plan, then look for a project the leaders are paying close attention to. One they have allocated significant resources to. A project with lofty objectives that people aren't sure they can achieve is an excellent opportunity for a champion. Figure out how Design Thinking can help the project succeed. Then use all your championing skills and **Hitch a Ride**.

There are four kinds of people in adopting an alternative approach. 1s: don't know about it. 2s: are aware but not yet convinced it's worth a try. 3s: are interested in trying. 4s: are trying it. Are the people in your part of the organization 1s and 2s? Are you struggling to make them aware and willing to try Design Thinking? Forget about them! **Go for the 3s**. In most organizations there are pockets of keeners willing to try new approaches. Maybe they are in a small department. Or a group with a progressive leader. Or a team in trouble searching for a better way. Seek them out. Become their ally. Collaborate with them using Design Thinking and show the 1s and 2s how it's done.

In organizations there is usually a center of gravity, a head office or a main plant or the dominant virtual team that holds most of the control. It's difficult to try new approaches in the center of gravity. The closer you are to center, the harder it is to break the bounds of its inertia and size. A champion can have a better chance of getting support where the pull isn't so strong. Try somewhere else. **Launch in a Satellite** office. They are less constrained by the forces at the center. Often they want to show what they are capable of. Put them in the focus of people back at head office by getting results using Design Thinking.

Unlike an established team, a task force is temporary. It is a group of people brought together to focus on a critical issue. Task forces are used for finding solutions to perplexing time-critical problems such as a response to a competitor's move, an impending regulatory change, or recovering from a natural disaster. Their focus is of the "we can't fail" nature – high risk and high profile. What a better place to showcase the power of Design Thinking. People are watching. They want to see results. Volunteer for a task force. Be their Design Thinking expert and **Take it to Task**.

Nature versus nurture is one of the oldest debates in psychology. What's more important – inherited traits or learned behaviors? In organizations, inherited ways of doing things become second nature, unquestioned and invisible. It is difficult to nurture new behaviors when they go against the very nature of your organization. How can you nurture alternative ways of working like Design Thinking when the force of that nature is so strong? Find areas of the organization that are not yet fully formed. Places where their nature is just emerging. Perhaps it's a new regional office or a new department being set up or a team forming to pursue an unfamiliar challenge. Make Design Thinking a part of their developing work processes. **Nurture a New Nature** in an emerging part of your organization.

There are formal, officially sanctioned projects. Then there are informal projects. Informal projects are often passion projects of ad hoc groups of people from across the organization. Like a green team working to make their office more environmentally sustainable, or volunteers working on a community service project. The good news is informal projects aren't subject to the formal rules of the organization. They are not under the same scrutiny and constraints. However, the rest of the organization is watching and rooting for them. Informal projects are a great place for people to get first-hand experience with Design Thinking without taking a lot of risk. So, **Go Informal**. Work some Design Thinking magic with passionate people. They'll go back to their formal projects knowing how Design Thinking works.

STRUT OUT

APPEAL TO THEIR BIG WHY!

ULTIMATE PULL

GET THEM PUMPED

FOMO

BASIC PLUS Premium

LEARN FOR THEMSELVES

"OMG, YOU KNOW WHAT HE'S LIKE!"

Vijay was clearly having little success. Again. If everyone was like me, they found his presentation off-putting if not down-right condescending. Vijay was a really smart guy, a Ph.D. Technology fascinated him. He was constantly discovering new ways he felt could make our training programs the most advanced in the industry.

This presentation was about his latest find. Maybe it was the next greatest thing, but his forceful selling turned all of us off. We weren't buying it. Over time, Vijay's lack of success in getting support had made him bitter and it showed. He was in a vicious cycle he couldn't seem to spin himself out of. The harder he pushed, the harder we resisted, the more frustrated he got. When he finished his presentation, I left immediately. I didn't want to engage with him.

You can imagine how I felt later that week when Jocelyn, my boss, told me she wanted Vijay to report to me! "Vijay is a brilliant guy. He has good ideas but needs help, Dan." she said. "OMG, you know what he's like, Jocelyn," I replied. Knowing I wasn't going to eagerly jump at the opportunity, Jocelyn suggested I have a call with Vijay. "Be frank with him. If it doesn't go well, I won't force you to accept." With very low expectations, I set up a call with Vijay.

During our call, it became apparent that Vijay was tired. Tired from all the effort he was spending pushing his ideas with no success. It was also apparent he had some ideas with potential. I got real with him. His approach had to change or we wouldn't be able to make it work. Vijay and I agreed to give it a try. We'd work together and get some of his ideas into practice. Meanwhile, the little voice in the back of my head was saying, "Man, you're gonna need all your collaboration skills you can muster to make this work!"

We got Jocelyn to give us a small budget to set up a "lab" (really just a closet to store the tech gadgets we cobbled together). We wanted to do some prototyping with real instructors in training programs with real customers. The instructors refused. Too risky. And the thought of dealing with Vijay was frankly unappealing to them. So, we ran our experiments ourselves in internal staff training programs. Not ideal, but we learned a lot. **And we knew we were on to something. The technology, used correctly, was dramatically improving the depth and pace of learning for the participants. The "used correctly" part became our next big issue.**

"Used correctly" meant the instructors had to be good at using the technologies. It also required changes in the way they interacted with the students. Realizing this, the instructors refused to even try. They were pros at what they did. No need to learn new ways. But we needed the instructors to put the technologies into practice. No amount of selling seemed to convince them.

However, one instructor, Christine, was intrigued. She turned out to be our lead user, working with us in the lab. She helped us refine the use of the technologies. We learned what it meant for the instructors, how to help them become more adept at using them by building on their current facilitation skills. Seeing Christine involved and not wanting to be left behind, other instructors began paying attention.

One day we were running another prototype training program. Bill from business development was giving a campus tour to representatives from a potential customer, a big management consulting firm. As they passed by the training room, they noticed we were up to something. Something very different. An unusual room setup and tech devices everywhere. "What's happening here?" they asked. Bill replied, "It's our lab. We were experimenting with new ways of using technology." Bill called Vijay and me out into the hallway and asked us to explain. We did.

Two weeks later Bill closed the deal with the management consulting firm. It was a BIG deal in many ways, one being they insisted all their training programs take place in the lab! They wanted only the latest and greatest for their staff. This meant instructors would need to use the technologies in all our campuses worldwide! The ultimate pull came from the customer. The instructors got pulled into using the technologies Vijay had been pushing for so long.

THOUGHTS?

THE HARDER I PUSH,
THE MORE PUSH BACK I GET.

Marketers have a couple of strategies for getting you to purchase their product. The push strategy is just that – pushing the product at you; banner ads or 25% off the first month subscription pop-ups. **The pull strategy is the opposite. They pull you into a relationship with their brand.** They blog helpful information or sponsor the social media influencers you follow. Both <u>push and pull</u> can be effective. But I find having a product pushed at me annoying.

 ## ATTRACTING BEATS SELLING.

Realizing for myself a product is the right solution for me is much more motivating. That's the power of intrinsic motivation over extrinsic motivation.

HMW... PULL INSTEAD OF PUSH?

If people are resisting your push for Design Thinking, try the pull instead. Get them to get themselves to want it.

STRUT OUT

Apple does it. Tesla does it. Fashion designers do it. With great fanfare, they reveal their cool new watches, cars and clothes. Why? Because they know the power of cool for attracting attention and driving desire. A great champion ploy is to make Design Thinking cool. Position it as an edgy, fresh way to get results. Work with other trendsetters in your organization. Show how they get results using Design Thinking. Or showcase the stunning visual artifacts Design Thinkers produce. Or make Design Thinking tantalizingly exclusive. By invitation only. Be careful to not overplay it, though. Bean bag chairs and wall to wall whiteboards are not sufficient. People can see fake cool a mile away. Cool is only cool if it can produce results. **Strut Out the Cool** of Design Thinking.

People work in organizations for different reasons. Some are driven by the mission. Others want personal growth and development. Others the comfort that comes from a steady income. Everyone has **Their BIG Why**. If they see Design Thinking as supporting it they'd be interested. So, find out their Big Why. Ask them what keeps them coming back day after day to the job they do. The real reason they work there. Then show them how taking up Design Thinking can help with their Big Why. How a deep understanding of the people you serve means a better chance of achieving the mission. Or the personal growth that comes from stretching to learn a new approach. Or how continual iteration of your service helps insure your organization's long-term viability. Go for the pull. Appeal to their Big Why.

As a Design Thinker, you might find the idea of mashing up Design Thinking and competition weird. You know the power of collaboration, that great ideas come from the interaction between people with different perspectives working together. But competition done right can motivate people to push themselves to higher levels. Achieving a personal best builds self-esteem and confidence. Competing can spur people to try new ways to win. Organizations are full of people up for a competitive challenge, who want to be winners. If you're having trouble getting people interested in Design Thinking, try getting them to compete. Can their team make the best attempt at using Design Thinking? Give them a challenge. Award a prize. Give away bragging rights. Use competition to **Get Them Pumped** and try Design Thinking.

Have you noticed subscription services offer three pricing levels; Basic/Plus/Premium? (Plus is often tagged as the most popular.) Each with increasing features and prices. Why? They want to give us options. They know we enjoy having choices. It makes us feel like we are in control. It's our decision to select one that best suits our interests, the one that is most beneficial for us. We are more likely to sign up when we have options. Only a few, though; having too many choices can be overwhelming. As a champion, you may find people who are interested in Design Thinking but reluctant to try. Options can be the pull you need. Offer them a few different ways to start. Maybe three ways to better understand their customers. Or four ways to prototype an idea they have. Or two ways to prioritize the possible service offerings. Help them understand the merits of each. Then leave it to them to select the one to try. Get them engaged by giving them the feeling of control.

There's nothing more motivating than customer demands. Organizations that ignore them do so at their peril. What if you could get your customers to demand your organization use Design Thinking? Maybe customers who use your service can demand it be used to better understand their unmet needs. Or funders demand that stakeholders of your non-profit help with a redesign of your programs. Sometimes it's hard for a champion to get customers to outright demand it. But try it anyway. A great fall back are proxies. Perhaps making the executives aware their clients are setting up their own design labs. Or your product managers that teenagers are designing their own video games. Or your sales folks that customers are leaving because the competitors are co-creating solutions with them. Customer demands and their proxies give champions the **Ultimate Pull**.

Fear of missing out (FOMO) is a motivator. Who wants to be the last to know? Who wants to be left behind? As a champion, use **FOMO** to attract and engage people. Make them feel like they have to know about it. They have to get Design Thinking or they'll be left out. Use every communication channel you can. Write blogs. Get featured in the company newsletter. Get interviewed on a podcast. Show how key players in the organization use Design Thinking. Make it feel like Design Thinking is everywhere, that they risk being left behind. Show that you can help them stay at the forefront. Play to their FOMO and pull them along.

You've just completed an awesome training program (let's say a Design Thinking workshop)! You're back at work excited to share what you learned, the possibilities you see. You wish you weren't the only one who attended the program. You try explaining the concepts, but you have trouble putting them into words they'll understand. You struggle to transfer your newfound passion to others. So, how can you get them to share your passion for Design Thinking? Have people learn it for themselves. Get people to use their training budgets to attend the workshop you attended. Or get your team to take part in an online course. Or watch a webinar series on Design Thinking together. Give a series of lunchtime lectures yourself. Smooth the way for them to **Learn for Themselves**.

"NOBODY IS LISTENING TO US MUSKETEERS."

We saw the world changing around us. Lina, VP of Market Research, was seeing shifts in retailing and consumer preferences. Kamal, VP of Advanced Technology, was seeing new sensing technologies that could alter the cost structure in our industry. And I was seeing the need to increase the sophistication of our designs. We called ourselves the Three Musketeers, heroically fighting to get others in our organization to see what we were seeing: an emerging, uncertain future with all its perils and opportunities.

We took every chance we could to raise awareness of the changes we were seeing – in strategic planning sessions, budgeting meetings, update meetings, and informal conversations with the executives. But people weren't paying attention. No reason to. We had a successful business with record sales and financial results. Why would the future be any different? But we knew with success comes the danger of complacency. We could see the world was changing. We weren't.

"Nobody's listening. We need to try something different," I said during one of our regular Musketeer commiseration sessions. "Let's try to engage people in a discussion about the future. Let's invite them to post what they think it might hold. Get them to share their perspectives." "Worth a try. Nobody is listening to us Musketeers," Lina and Kamal replied. So, that's what we did.

After a few days, we looked at what they had posted. It confirmed our suspicions – people had a scary view of the future. Things would continue to grow at a steady pace; the competitors would remain predictable; their work would stick to the usual routine; the world would look pretty much the same, only slightly better. Augh!

One day Lina called Kamal and me. "I've found something interesting," she said. "Consultants who facilitate discussions on the future." The hair on the back of my neck went up immediately. I had seen too many consultants take our ideas, present them back to us, then charge us a fortune. Why get consultants involved? After my blood pressure dropped back to near normal, I listened to what she had to say.

"They're different. They don't come in and tell you about the future. They facilitate a dialogue between our leaders and experts in areas like consumer trends, retailing, advanced technologies and design." *Now this sounds interesting*, I thought. "We select the experts we know the executives will respect," she continued. "Plus, a couple of our own ringers. During the session they will present a provocative picture of the future. Anyone can question and challenge them. Better they get their answers from experts, than from us. After all, we are only Musketeers."

Lina, Kamal and I scraped together the budget and hired the consultants. They facilitated the dialogue session with our execs and managers. Their presentations were provocative. Lively and heated discussions resulted. A dramatic shift in our collective view of the future happened right in front of our eyes.

Before adjourning, the execs and managers collectively created a 10-year **Future Map**. It depicted a dramatically different future than they had previously imagined, illustrating trends and discontinuities we needed to prepare for. The Future Map became a tool used in our annual planning. Over time, investments in advanced technologies, new retail distribution channels and expanded design capability ensured our success continued.

IDEAS?

 ## I CAN'T SEEM TO CONVINCE PEOPLE.

My friend Noelle Dye, a pioneer of design research, says, "Your voice gets smaller when you go inside." Over the years she has worked both as a consultant and employee for many cool startups. She's been the expert both inside and outside of companies. She knows people listen to outside voices over the more familiar ones inside.

It seems when we are close to someone we tend to tune them out. We think we know what they are going to say. Whereas an unfamiliar voice can have an air of authority. An assumed expertise based on outside experience. A seemingly unbiased perspective worth paying attention to.

 ## OTHERS CAN BE MORE CONVINCING THAN YOU.

Even if your message is the same, the outsider's is the one that gets heard. Sometimes it's best for a champion to let others be the champion.

HMW... LET OTHERS DO IT?

Step away from the microphone and orchestrate their voices. Let others do it.

_____

_____

_____

_____

_____

_____

In the old days, a ringer was a fast horse secretly substituted for a similar looking but slower one in a race. A dubious act, for sure. But these days a ringer means a highly skilled person brought in to supplement a sports team. Someone who can lift the team's chances of winning. If a team is struggling with Design Thinking but not listening to your advice, **Bring in a Ringer**. Get another talented Design Thinker assigned to the team. They can come from inside or outside of your organization. It's up to you if you want to keep their expertise secret or not! Let a ringer make the team a winner.

As humans, we tend to respond more favorably to those in our own group. Psychologists call this innate human trait ingroup bias. The dark side of ingroup bias is prejudice and exclusion. But we can use the tendency to view others in our group positively to champion Design Thinking. Are you having trouble persuading people not like you? Maybe engineers in the technical department. Or the accountants in the finance group. Or the fund raisers on the development team. Find someone like-minded. Someone with their background who is a Design Thinking believer. Get them to be the champion in that group. **Enlist the Like-Minded** to do it for you.

Who do senior leaders ask when they need advice on a challenging problem? Consultants? Internal staff? Academics? Maybe. But whose advice do they trust the most? Other senior leaders. People in their position who have faced the same uncertainty. Find a senior leader from another organization who has embraced Design Thinking. Maybe someone in your community of practice, your LinkedIn group or your business association can point you to a leader who has led the successful adoption of Design Thinking in their organization. Someone who can speak to the trials, tribulations and rewards of doing it. Set up a dialogue between them and your senior leaders. Let **Senior 2 Senior** conversations do the championing for you.

Not getting a lot of traction? Feeling like you don't have the stature to move Design Thinking forward in your organization? Don't get disillusioned. Sometimes the best way to be a champion is to be a sidekick. Be the Hermione instead of the Harry. The one who solves the riddles, figures out the solutions, and executes the plans while accompanying the hero on the quest. Find a person with status in your organization. Maybe a senior leader or someone widely respected. Someone who has the attention of others. Become a duo and work together. Being a champion sometimes means you step out of the spotlight and **Be the Sidekick**.

Teams learning Design Thinking on a project often have to sort things out for themselves. They have to muddle through defining their roles, figuring out how to work together, and how to apply unfamiliar methods. As the lone Design Thinker on the project, others can see you as the expert. They can also see you as biased and pushing your agenda. You are a champion, but you may not have the standing to move the team along in the most efficient way. Engage a Design Thinking coach. A coach can nudge the team in the right direction. They can ask the right questions to keep the team moving and share their expertise in applying Design Thinking, all from a position of outside objectivity. Championship teams have great coaches who have played the game themselves. **Hire a Design Thinking Coach** and let them spur the team along to the win.

A person who has faced a daunting challenge and overcome it inspires us. Someone who has summited Everest or run 25 marathons in 25 days or prevailed over a disadvantaged childhood to attain success in life. Their stories can build our confidence that we too can do great things. There are thousands of TEDx videos of people who have overcome challenges to inspire us. But most inspiring is being able to interact directly with them, to get their answers to our unique and personal questions. Hearing first-hand from someone who's **Been There Done That** is a powerful motivator. Try setting up and hosting an expert panel. A panel of people who have succeeded with Design Thinking. Invite the resisters, dissenters and skeptics. Let them get their questions answered by people who have done it. Let experts who have been there done that remove their doubt and get them inspired.

We have pondered a bunch of How Might We's and looked at a raft of sticky notes of practical ideas for you to consider. Some are well suited for you in your organization and some less so. Some will require you to champion boldly. Some will take a lighter touch.

As I have said, championing Design Thinking is a marathon, not a sprint. You will face resistance. You will have little wins and an occasional big one. I certainly did.

When I reflect on all the stories, I ask myself the question, what kept me going? Was it the desire to create cool designs? Was it the challenge of getting people to see things my way? Was it my responsibility to help organizations succeed? Was it an unrelenting curiosity to learn and try new things? And the answer is yes. Each of those kept me going, but only for a time. Their ability to drive me would wax and wane.

I now realize what sustained me over the long haul was a much bigger reason; my deeply held belief that human-centered design can help us address the complex challenges we face in this world. Our organizations, communities, and society at large need Design Thinkers like you to make a difference in things that really matter. That's what has kept me going.

_____

_____

_____

_____

_____

_____

_____

 ## I HAVE TO STAY MOTIVATED.

My ultimate goal kept me going. What is your goal in trying to get your organization to embrace Design Thinking? Are you passionate about becoming customer focused? Or breaking down the infuriating silos that slow innovation down? Or helping others get unstuck and use their creative abilities? Or impacting some of the world's most wicked problems?

 ## YOUR BIG WHY WILL SUSTAIN YOU.

When faced with setbacks, pause and remind yourself why this is so important to you.

HMW... ALWAYS KNOW OUR BIG WHY?

Stay positive and remember your efforts — no matter how strenuous and tiring — are focused on your BIG why.

Knowing your higher purpose, your BIG why for championing Design Thinking can keep you going in the face of obstacles. Nietzsche, the influential philosopher, said, "He who has a why can endure any how." Find your BIG why by using the **Five Why's**. Start with the statement "I want to champion Design Thinking in my organization." Then ask yourself why? Why do you want to champion Design Thinking? Write your answer down. Now ask yourself why do you want to that. Repeat this four more times by asking yourself why for each previous answer. Then look over your 5 answers and select the one that best expresses your BIG why. Keep it front and center to drive you.

As a Design Thinker, you know the power of visualization. Illustrating the future success of a new idea is a great tool for getting support for it. So, ask yourself, "What will success look like for my organization when I have succeeded as a Design Thinking champion?" Having your own vision can activate your creativity, help you recognize opportunities and attract people to support your quest. Create a **Splash Page Mockup** to make your vision visible. Imagine your organization has been profiled by a major news site for the success it has achieved by using Design Thinking. Mock up the splash page that features the story of your organization's impact, the difference it has made in the world. Keep this vision in front of you. Refer back to it often. Share it with others.

Why are you championing Design Thinking? What's in it for you personally? Is it the way you want to work every day? Is it the creative environment you want to be in? Is it about the people you want to collaborate with? Is it the innovative ideas you know you will create? Imagine what it will feel like when you succeed. Having a dream is a good thing. Just like in idea generation, your subconscious can work magic. Get it silently searching for creative ways to make your dream come true. Give it a picture to work with. Create a **Vision Board** of your desired future, a collage of images that express your Design Thinking dream. Then leave the rest up to your subconscious!

May 6, 2021

From: Dan Buchner
Re: Onward!
To: Design Thinking Champions
cc: Would-Be Design Thinking Champions

Hey you!

My hope is this book will up your game as a Design Thinking champion, helping you be the change you want to see. I hope the stories in this book inspire you to strive to be brave and bold. I hope you found guidance in the principles to imagine new ways that work for you. Ultimately, I hope you found practical ideas you can act on.

While you face challenges as a champion, there are ways to make Design Thinking a reality in your organization. My hope is this book has given you a window into some of them. Now the rest is up to you.

You have the passion and creativity to overcome the frustrations and resistance. Your organization needs you. I need you. And the world needs you. The potential of Design Thinking won't be realized without champions like you.

Onward!

DAN BUCHNER

Dan@praktikel.io
www.praktikel.io/hmw-book

GLOSSARY OF TERMS (from a Design Thinker's perspective)

#

70-20-10 Rule – A rule derived from research by The Center for Creative Leadership. It states that there are 3 types of experiences needed for leaders to learn and grow: 70% challenging experiences and assignments, 20% developmental relationships such as coaching and mentoring, and 10% coursework and training. *Morgan McCall, Michael M Lombardo, Robert W Eichinger, "The Career Architect Development Planner," Lominger, 1996.*

A

Affinity Clusters – A Design Thinking method for grouping like items together to reveal themes and patterns. Individual ideas from brainstorming or data from field research are written on sticky notes. Related stickies are then moved next to each other forming clusters. Reviewing the clusters can reveal hidden meanings and insights to help Design Thinkers imagine innovative new concepts.

After-Action Review – A structured debriefing process for analyzing what happened, why it happened and what can be done better next time. It was originally developed by the US army to compare the intended vs. actual results achieved. Businesses have adopted it to build cultures of accountability by having people examine and learn from their experiences.

Agile & Agile Sprints – Agile Methodology is a project management process, originally used for software development. Cross-functional teams collaborate to discover customer requirements and evolve solutions. Their work is broken down into a series of "sprints", each sprint building on the previous ones. The Agile Methodology values human communication and feedback, adapting to change and producing working results.

B

BHAG – The idea of the Big Hairy Audacious Goal was conceptualized in the book, "*Built to Last: Successful Habits of Visionary Companies*" by James Collins and Jerry Porras. A BHAG is a long-term goal so outrageous it might not even be possible to achieve. They are used to create a sense of urgency and encourage bold thinking inside of organizations. "Aim for the stars so if you miss you land on the moon," sums up the purpose of a BHAG.

Brainstorming – A method used by groups to generate a large number of ideas in a short period of time. It was developed by Alex Osborn, the American advertising executive, to produce original ideas and a wide range of options for carefully defined problems. The rules of brainstorming include deferring judgement, encouraging wild ideas, building on the ideas of others, and going for quantity. These rules allow those participating in a brainstorming session the freedom to contribute ideas they would not normally consider.

Building Trust – Leading trust expert, Dr. Darryl Stickle's research shows "higher trust levels lead to higher levels of performance, followership and profitability." To build trust with someone you must reduce their perceived uncertainty and vulnerability — their perceived risk. When their perceived risk is higher than their level of risk tolerance they will not trust you.

Bullseye Diagram – A simple tool used to prioritize items in order of importance. Like a bullseye, the most valuable space is in the center circle. The most important items are placed there. The middle ring is for medium priority items, while the lower priority items are placed in the outer ring.

Business Model Canvas – A template for developing and documenting business models. It is a visual description of a firm's value proposition, customers, infrastructure and finances. A Business Model Canvas is often created by a group of people to explore the potential of a new business.

C

Change Management – A structured process for implementing change within an organization. It is used to facilitate the transition to new ways of working while maximizing the chances people will adopt them. Change management practices work to move people past their inherent resistance of change and embrace the new ways of working.

Community of Practice (CoP) – A group of people who share a common interest in something they do. Their aim is to learn how to do it better by learning from each other. Members share their experiences and knowledge to collectively advance their capabilities. CoPs are used within organizations to spread best practices.

Concept – Design Thinkers generally refer to a concept as an early and not yet fully formed idea. Think concept car – a car that represents an idea of what the car might be in the future but is not yet in production. A concept is described in enough detail so others can understand and respond to it. However, it does not contain all the details needed to make it a reality.

Creative Matrix – A structure for rapidly generating large number of ideas at the intersection of discrete categories. A Creative Matrix is set up with the columns representing categories related to people and the rows representing categories of possible enablers for implementing the ideas generated. A group of people use the Creative Matrix to generate ideas using the rules of brainstorming. However, unlike conventional brainstorming, generating ideas using a Creative Matrix is done in silence to encourage everyone to participate.

D

Design Critique – A process for obtaining feedback to improve an idea or concept. A Design Critique involves gathering a small group of people, sharing the idea and asking for their feedback. Unlike a typical presentation, the purpose of a Design Critique is not to sell the idea but to gather as much feedback as possible.

Design Thinking – A practice for developing solutions in service of people. Teams use the iterative process to understand people, challenge assumptions, redefine problems, and prototype and test possible solutions. The aim is to produce innovations that are desirable for people and feasible and viable for the organization providing the solutions.

Design Thinking Coach – A professional with experience in the hands-on application of Design Thinking and the skills of helping others learn through experience. Design Thinking Coaches often work with individuals and teams on real projects, helping them develop their Design Thinking capabilities through guided practice.

Design Thinking Process – While there are many models of the Design Thinking Process the most common is the 5-phase process from the d-school at Stanford University. 1. Empathize – understanding users and their needs. 2. Define – based on this understanding, define the big user problem that needs to be solved. 3. Ideate – generate a set of creative ideas that might solve that problem. 4. Prototype – turn those ideas into tangible models that people can try and evaluate. 5. Test – Run experiments with the prototypes to learn about the pros and cons of the ideas.

Diffusion of Innovation Theory – Developed by E. M. Rogers to explain how a new product or idea spreads and gets adopted within a specific population. It describes how some people are more apt to adopt an innovation than others. He outlines the 5 main factors that influence the adoption: relative advantage, compatibility, complexity, triability and observability. *Everett Rogers, "Diffusion of Innovations", The Free Press of Glencoe, 1962.*

DiSC – The DiSC® behavioral assessment tool is based on the theory by psychologist William Moulton Marston. It focuses on 4 personality traits: dominance, inducement, submission and compliance. It is used to reduce conflict and improve working relationships by helping individuals understand themselves and others.

Discover Phase – The first phase of the Design Thinking process, also known as the Empathize Phase. During this phase, teams use a variety of qualitative research techniques to develop a deep understanding of customers' behaviors and attitudes to uncover the real problem to be solved.

Double Diamond Model – A Design Thinking approach developed by the British Design Council. The model consists of 4 Phases: 1. Discover – insights into the real problem 2. Define – the area to focus on 3. Develop – potential solutions, and 4. Deliver – solutions that work. The first two phases make up the first diamond – exploring the problem space. The last 2 phases make up the second diamond – exploring the solution space. Moving through the 2 diamonds, teams use divergent thinking to explore options then convergent thinking to focus their decisions.

E

Empathy Map – A template for capturing a customer's behavior and attitudes. Teams use an Empathy Map to record what the customer thinks, feels, says and does, as well as the pain they have with current solutions and the gain they wish to get from new solutions. This allows teams to uncovered insights to guide the development of innovative new solutions.

Envisioning – A visualization practice used to imagine new possibilities. In the Define Phase of the Design Thinking process, envisioning is used to explore potential future concepts for addressing a problem identified in the Discover Phase.

Ethnographic Research – The research approach used by anthropologists to understand, interrupt and describe a particular culture. The ethnographic research methods are used in their fieldwork in the culture being studied. Design Thinkers have adopted many of these methods to develop a deep understanding of the people they are designing for.

Expert Interview – An interview method where the interviewee is an expert in their field. Expert Interviews are used to gather information from people who are not direct customers. These experts have detailed knowledge that might be useful for a team's project. Expert interviews can take many forms: one-on-one, virtual, formal or informal.

Extreme Users – The users at the ends of a spectrum of users. The normal distribution of users of a product or service is often a bell curve. The bulk of the users are in the middle with the extreme users on either end. At one end they can be people who never use a product and at the other end fanatical users. Extreme users' needs are amplified. They may have found novel ways to use the product. Or the product doesn't meet their needs at all. By exploring how extreme users use or don't use a product, teams can find opportunities to innovate.

F

Fail Fast Fail Often – A mantra of Silicon Valley that espouses the notion that one learns from trying and not succeeding. Or, better to try and fail then not try at all. Design Thinkers adopted this idea to describe the iterative nature of the Design Process of rapidly prototyping and testing ideas. Fail fast and Fail Often can be seen by leaders in organizations as a risky approach as failure is not considered an option.

Fishbone Diagram – A cause-and-effect diagram is used to identify the reasons for failures or defects. Also, known as the Ishikawa Diagram it was developed by Kaoru Ishikawa, a pioneer of quality management. It looks like a fish skeleton where the problem is the head and the causes of the problem the bones leading to the spine. By creating a Fishbone Diagram, teams can explore the causes and find possible solutions.

Five Why's – A technique for getting to the root cause of a problem. Teams begin with a clear definition of a problem then proceed to ask and answer Why? five times to arrive at a probable cause. The Five Why's was invented by Toyota to uncover the root cause of production process problems. Once the true cause is uncovered, teams take corrective measures to avoid the recurrence of the problem. Here we are using the Five Why's to get to the root motivation of a Design Thinking champion.

Force Field Map – A diagram used to analyze the forces acting for and against a desired change within organizations. Developed by social scientist Kurt Lewin, Force Field Maps are used to understand the forces acting on individuals or teams. With this understanding, teams can develop ways to amplify the forces working for the change and reduce the forces working against it.

Fuckup Night - A global movement where stories about business failure are shared monthly. The organization's motto, "We Live Life Without Filters," speaks to their objective of helping business people learn from each other's failures. www.fuckupnights.com

Future Map – A graphical presentation of a future scenario including anticipated events, trends and discontinuities. Teams build future maps to explore and build alignment on possible future conditions that need to be considered in developing new products, services or business strategies.

H

Hermione – The popular character in the Harry Potter books. Author J. K. Rowling calls her a "very logical, upright and good" character who uses her quick wit and extensive knowledge to aid Harry when he faces dire situations.

How Might We question (HMW) – Harvard Business Review calls them, "The Secret Phrase Top Innovators Use." An HMW question is a format for framing problems that invites broad exploration of new ideas. The 'How" and the "Might" suggests a solution is possible. The "We" reminds us that innovating is a collaborative undertaking. HMW questions are aspirational goals that may not be achieved but serve to expand thinking and fuel idea generation.

I

Idea Bank – A repository, usually a website, where people share, discuss and advance ideas. Idea Banks are used by organizations to gather and vet suggestions for improvements to products, services, and processes.

Importance Difficulty Matrix – A 2X2 matrix used to establish priorities. A relative ranking of the importance of items is done on the x axis, while relative difficulty is on the y axis. Teams using the matrix must first determine and agree on how importance and difficulty will be assessed. Doing the relative ranking of importance first without regard to the items' difficulty, then doing the difficulty ranking, is considered best practice.

Ingroup Bias – The tendency to favor one's own group over groups of different people. Ingroup bias can lead to favoritism and, in its extreme, prejudice and exclusion.

Insights – Jonahan Dalton, CEO of Thrive Thinking has a multi-faceted definition of an insight that is useful for Design Thinkers:

- An unrecognized fundamental human truth.

- A new way of viewing the world that causes us to reexamine existing conventions and challenge the status quo.

- A penetrating observation about human behavior that results in seeing consumers from a fresh perspective.

- A discovery about the underlying motivations that drive people's actions.

Derived from data gathered in the Discover Phase, Insights are used in the Define Phase to arrive at the real problem to solve. *Jonathan Dalton, "What is an insight? the 5 Principles of Insight Definition",* https://thrivethinking.com/2016/03/28/what-is-insight-definition/

Interests vs Positions – 2 different approaches to negotiating. Interest-based negotiation works to produce a win-win result for both parties. Position-based negotiation is a zero-sum approach resulting in one party winning and the other losing.

Interviews – A research technique for gathering information through direct dialogue. Design Thinkers interview people to develop an understanding of their attitudes and behaviors to uncover unmet needs and desires. This type of interviewing is conversational in nature; the person being interviewed "leads" the conversation often to unexpectedly useful places.

J

Journey Maps – A graphical representation of a person's interactions and experiences with a product or service over time. Teams use Journey Maps to document and understand the customer's experience from their customer's perspective.

K

Key Performance Indicators (KPIs) – A set of measures for individual, team or organizational performance. KPIs are designed to focus and manage the main drivers of their success. In many organizations people's compensation is tied to achieving their KPIs. This links individual performance to the overall performance of the organization.

L

Landscape – A graphical representation of all the elements of a system. Design Thinkers create landscape maps to develop an understanding of all the elements of the project, target market and use case of a product or service.

Lead User – A person who faces an unmet need long before the general population and who will benefit from it being addressed. Lead users are important to innovators as they develop their own solutions. Paying attention to lead users can help teams develop new products and services for future needs of the general population.

Loss Avoidance Bias – The tendency to prefer avoiding a loss over getting an equivalent gain. Identified by Amos Tversky and Daniel Kahneman, this bias suggests we experience losses twice as powerfully as gains. Better to position a new approach as a way to avoid a loss than to achieve a gain. *Daniel Kahneman, Amos Tversky, "Prospect Theory: An Analysis of Decision Under Risk," Econonmetrica, 1979.*

Loyal Skeptic – A role to be played on a team. Loyal skeptics are "loyal" to the cause of the team but unafraid to play the skeptic by asking difficult questions. They help the team avoid group think and unexplored options. They are not Loyal "Cynics" who are an irritant to the team's progress.

LUMA Institute – A global education company that empowers people to be more innovative by applying the discipline of human-centered design. LUMA has created a framework to allow people to select the best design method to use for a challenge they face. LUMA offers expertly led Human-Centered Design training programs and practitioner and facilitation certifications.

M

MBTI® – An assessment used to make a person aware of their preferences in how they perceive the world and make decisions. The Myers Briggs Type Indicator is the most widely used personality test in the world. It is used to make people aware of their preferences so they can better communicate and relate to others.

Medium is the Message – Marshall McLuhan, the communication theorist said, "It is impossible to understand social and cultural changes without a knowledge of the workings of media." For McLuhan the medium is more important than the message it conveys. New methods of communicating change the way people behave. *Marshall McLuhan, "Understanding Media: The Extensions of Man," McGraw-Hill, 1964.*

O

Organizational Change – The practice of moving an organization from a current state to a preferred state. The need for organizational change can arise from competitive actions, technology advancements, and ownership changes. These necessitate major shifts in the organization's personnel, processes, strategy and culture. Because people can be hesitant or resistance to change, managing an organizational change involves reducing their anxiety and making the transition process understandable and achievable.

P

Personas – A description of a made-up person that represents the needs, experiences, behaviors and goals of a specific set of customers. Based on research done by design teams, Personas are used to ensure solutions being designed are appropriate and desirable for those customers.

Pivot – The act of moving to plan B when plan A has been shown not to work. This term is popular in the start-up world. Entrepreneurs are expected to quickly pivot to a new or modified business plan if their current one isn't working.

Prototype and Test – An approach to get feedback on a concept or idea. A key principle of Design Thinking is building to learn. This is accomplished by prototyping and testing early and often during the design process. Models of the idea are made and tested with customers to learn about its merits and shortcomings. This is a low cost, low risk way for teams to quickly refine their idea.

Push and Pull – 2 strategies used by marketers to move a customer from awareness to purchase. The Push strategy involves pushing their customers to purchase by, for instance, offering discounts, or limited time offers. The Pull strategy involves pulling customers to purchase by helping them develop a relationship with the brand. Examples of pull tactics include providing helpful information and endorsements by third party influencers. Both can be effective strategies depending on the preferences of the target customers.

R

Reframing (A Problem) – Restating a problem from a different perspective. One of the most powerful Design Thinking tools is reframing the problem to address. Often the initial problem statement is narrow and assumes a particular path to a solution. Reframing the problem can open up the possible solution set to a variety of novel ideas. Turning a problem statement into an aspirational How Might We question is an effective way to reframe a problem.

Retrospective – A structured review of a team's past performance with the aim of improving it in the future. At the end of an Agile Sprint or project phase, teams access what worked well and what might be improved in the next sprint or phase.

Risk/Reward Chart – A scatter plot used to assess the risk and reward profile of an investment portfolio. A set of individual investments are plotted by their average returns — Rewards — versus the average volatility of the price of the investment — Risk. Other versions of Risk/Reward charts can be created to assess the range of options before making critical decisions.

Role Play – A method to prototype the delivery of a service or other in-person interactions. Playing the roles of people involved in the experience, team members act it out. This allows the team to refine their idea by uncovering its merits and shortcoming.

Rose/Thorn/Bud – A method for categorizing items as positive (rose), negative (thorn) and having potential (bud). This versatile technique was originated by the Boy Scouts of America. It is used in many ways by Design Thinkers including making sense of research data and soliciting feedback on ideas.

S

Self-Assessment – A tool used by individuals to discover their interests, aptitudes, personality type, values, and performance. DiSC® and MBTI® are 2 popular self-assessments used in organizations to help people identify their strengths and better leverage them to improve communications and interpersonal relationships.

Sense Making – The process Design Thinkers use to interpret and give meaning to research data gained in the Define Phase. Sense making involves discovering patterns, relationships and unexpected connections. By making sense of these, teams arrive at insights that allow them to frame the real problem to solve in the Define Phase.

Six Sigma – A process improvement methodology focused on decreasing process variation by enhancing process control. Originated by Motorola engineer Bill Smith, Six Sigma techniques and tools are used by organizations to improve the quality of their products and services as well as profits and employee engagement.

Splash Page Mockup – A future success story of a concept in the form of a prototype website landing page. Splash Page Mockups are used to create excitement for the concept's benefits and potential.

Stage Gate (Process) – A project management process that uses a series of phases or stages each separated by decision making points called stage gates. To pass through a stage gate a project team must show that the project meets or exceeds pre-established criteria. This allows for the monitoring and control of the progress outcomes and costs. Organizations use the Stage Gate process on development and improvement projects.

Stakeholder Map –A graphical representation of a network of people involved in and impacted by a system. Design Thinkers create Stakeholder Maps to build an understanding of the people they need to consider in developing solutions. Stakeholder Maps are not organization charts. They are an expansive map of individuals or individual roles showing their relationships and interactions relating to a problem to be solved.

Stand Ups – Short, often daily meetings where team members share their progress and seek help addressing any challenges they face in completing their upcoming tasks. Some teams conduct these meetings while standing up to encourage them to keep on topic and keep it brief.

Standard Operating Procedure (SOP) – Step by step instructions for successfully executing routine operations within an organization. SOPs are used to ensure efficiency, consistency, quality of output and compliance with laws and regulations.

Statistical Regression Analysis – A mathematical modelling process for estimating the relationship between a dependent variable and one or more independent variables. Regression Analysis is used to determine which of the independent variables have the most impact on the dependent variable. They are also used to find trends in a set of data.

Sticky Notes – A generic term for 3M Post-it® notes. Design Thinkers are avid users of Sticky Notes, in both paper and digital forms, for capturing ideas and succinctly visualizing data. Each annotated Sticky Note is a data point and many make a data set. Because Sticky Notes can be easily arranged and rearranged, teams use them to explore patterns and relationships within a data set.

Storyboards – A sequence of illustrations and information describing a story or experience over a period of time. Comic strips and graphic novels are forms of Storyboards. Design Thinkers use Storyboards to obtain feedback on new service concepts and use scenarios of new product concepts.

StrengthsFinder® – A self-assessment from the Gallup Organization used to help individuals identify their top 5 strengths from the 4 domains of Strategic Thinking, Relationship Building, Influence and Executing. Knowing their strengths, individuals can build on them and improve their performance.

T

TEDx – A local gathering where speakers present "ideas worth sharing" in under 18 minutes each. Organizers of a TEDx select interesting themes and compelling speakers for select audiences. Thousands of TEDx talks can be viewed at www.TED.com/talks

Thumbnail Sketching – The drawing of small rough sketches (with no corrections) of an idea. They are often done on sticky notes using a fine tipped marker. Design Thinkers use Thumbnail Sketching to quickly visualize and communicate ideas.

Triggers (Emotional) – Memories, events or experiences that cause a strong reflexive emotional response. These responses are hard to control as they can be instinctive. Neuroscientist Dr. David Rock, states we can be triggered when we perceive threats to our physical and social well-being. Dealing with emotional triggers involves being mindful of the situations that initiate them then adapting your thinking and behavior to mitigate the effect of the trigger. *David Rock, "Scarf: A Brain-Based Model for Collaborating with and Influencing Others," NeuroLeadership Institute, 2008.*

Triple Bottom Line – An accounting framework used to evaluate the performance of an organization against 3 indicators; profit — financial, people — social, and planet — environmental. Environmentalists and social justice advocates have pushed organizations to adopt the Triple Bottom Line framework. Instead of focusing solely on profit and shareholder value, organizations use it to evaluate the long term impact of their decisions on society and the environment.

U

Use Case – A specific scenario describing how a customer might use a product or service. Use cases help teams understand the problems customers might face that then can be addressed with creative solutions.

UX (User Experience) – The process used to design the entire experience a user has when acquiring and using a product or service. UX designers look at such things as ease of use, perception of value, and utility to create products and services that will result in positive feelings of the users.

V

Values Audit – A survey conducted to assess how well people are living up to the stated values of their organization. A Values Audit provides leaders with an accurate reflection of the health of the culture of their organization. It can identify disconnects between the stated values and "how things actually get done around here". This allows leaders to take appropriate corrective actions. It can also show where the values are being strongly applied and should be encouraged.

Vision Board – A collage of images and affirmations illustrating a person's aspirations. People create Vision Boards to inspire and motive them to work to achieve their dreams.

Voice of the Customer – The feedback customers give on their expectations and experiences with a product, service and brand. Organizations use this data to direct their efforts to improve their product and services, drive customer loyalty and increase sales.

W

Walk-a-Mile Immersions – A method used by Design Thinkers to experience a product or service from the user's perspective. They put themselves in the user's shoes to uncover problems and opportunities only first-hand experience can reveal. With this new-found understanding new innovative solutions can be developed.

Waterfall (Model) – A project management process consisting of a linear series of phases where each phase is dependent on the completion of the previous one. The Waterfall Process is used on large complex engineering and software projects requiring the sequencing of specialized skills.

Wicked Problems – Problems that are nearly impossible to solve. Due to their complexity, ambiguity and changing requirements, the causes of Wicked Problems are difficult to even recognize. Unlike other types of problems, they do not have a single solution. Often in trying to solve a Wicked Problem, new problems are created. *C. West Churchman, "Wicked Problems," Management Science, 1967.*

Y

Yes And – An improv technique adopted by Design Thinkers to build on other's ideas. Responding to an idea with "Yes And" instead of "no" or "yes but" creates an openness to moving the idea forward, modifying it in a positive way or generating totally new unexpected ideas.

A version of this Affinity Clusters page is available for download at https://praktikel.io

ˈprɑktɪkəl
ideas for the real world

DAN BUCHNER
Design Thinking Champion
CEO & Founder, PRAKTIKEL Inc.

Dan Buchner is an award-winning designer, leadership facilitator, educator, and author. He draws on his practical experiences in business and life to shift thinking, transform perspectives, and inspire action. Dan brings the practice of Design Thinking to the intersection of innovation, leadership and organizational change. Dan has held leadership positions at Moen Inc., Continuum Innovation, The Center for Creative Leadership and Banff Centre for Arts and Creativity. He has worked with leading businesses, non-profits, governments, and universities including PepsiCo, Proctor & Gamble, Rockefeller Foundation, Texas A&M University, and USAID.

Dan's Design Thinking journey began decades ago in Canada and has taken him to 35 countries around the globe.

'prɑktikəl
Ideas for the real world